# When You Have to Go to Prison:

## A Complete Guide for You and Your Family

### By Margaret R. Kohut, MSW

*Certified Criminal Justice Specialist*

*Certified Criminal Justice Addiction Specialist*

*Clinically Certified Forensic Counselor*

*Master Addiction Counselor*

*Certified Forensic Addiction Examiner*

*Clinically Certified Domestic
Violence Counselor, Level 3*

# When You Have to Go to Prison: A Complete Guide for You and Your Family

Copyright © 2011 by Atlantic Publishing Group, Inc.
1405 SW 6th Ave. • Ocala, Florida 34471 • 800-814-1132 • 352-622-1875–Fax
Web site: www.atlantic-pub.com • E-mail: sales@atlantic-pub.com
SAN Number: 268-1250

Library of Congress Cataloging-in-Publication Data

Kohut, Margaret R.
  When you have to go to prison : a complete guide for you and your family / by Margaret R. Kohut.
      p. cm.
  Includes bibliographical references and index.
  ISBN-13: 978-1-60138-385-3 (alk. paper)
  ISBN-10: 1-60138-385-1 (alk. paper)
  1. Prisoners--United States--Life skills guides. 2. Prisons--United States. 3. Imprison-
ment--United States. 4. Criminal justice, Administration of--United States. 5. Prisoners'
families--United States. I. Title.
  HV9471.K64 2010
  365'.60973--dc22
                            2009054425

BOOK MANAGER: Kimberly Fulscher • FRONT & BACK COVER DESIGN: Holly Marie Gibbs
PEER REVIEWER: Marilee Griffin • EDITORIAL INTERN: Shannon McCarthy
INTERIOR DESIGN: T.L. Price • tlpricefreelance@gmail.com

Printed on Recycled Paper

Printed in the United States

We recently lost our beloved pet "Bear," who was not only our best and dearest friend but also the "Vice President of Sunshine" here at Atlantic Publishing. He did not receive a salary but worked tirelessly 24 hours a day to please his parents. Bear was a rescue dog that turned around and showered myself, my wife, Sherri, his grandparents  Jean, Bob, and Nancy, and every person and animal he met (maybe not rabbits) with friendship and love. He made a lot of people smile every day.

We wanted you to know that a portion of the profits of this book will be donated to The Humane Society of the United States. *–Douglas & Sherri Brown*

---

The human-animal bond is as old as human history. We cherish our animal companions for their unconditional affection and acceptance. We feel a thrill when we glimpse wild creatures in their natural habitat or in our own backyard.

Unfortunately, the human-animal bond has at times been weakened. Humans have exploited some animal species to the point of extinction.

The Humane Society of the United States makes a difference in the lives of animals here at home and worldwide. The HSUS is dedicated to creating a world where our relationship with animals is guided by compassion. We seek a truly humane society in which animals are respected for their intrinsic value, and where the human-animal bond is strong.

Want to help animals? We have plenty of suggestions. Adopt a pet from a local shelter, join The Humane Society and be a part of our work to help companion animals and wildlife. You will be funding our educational, legislative, investigative and outreach projects in the U.S. and across the globe.

Or perhaps you'd like to make a memorial donation in honor of a pet, friend or relative? You can through our Kindred Spirits program. And if you'd like to contribute in a more structured way, our Planned Giving Office has suggestions about estate planning, annuities, and even gifts of stock that avoid capital gains taxes.

Maybe you have land that you would like to preserve as a lasting habitat for wildlife. Our Wildlife Land Trust can help you. Perhaps the land you want to share is a backyard— that's enough. Our Urban Wildlife Sanctuary Program will show you how to create a habitat for your wild neighbors.

So you see, it's easy to help animals. And The HSUS is here to help.

**THE HUMANE SOCIETY**
**OF THE UNITED STATES.**

**2100 L Street NW • Washington, DC 20037 • 202-452-1100**
**www.hsus.org**

# Table of Contents

# Foreword

Hindsight is 20/20. This statement is typically made after the act. The deed is done, you've been charged and sentenced, and now it is time to prepare yourself and your loved ones for the consequences thereafter. *When You Have to go to Prison: A Complete Guide for You and Your Family* will help steer you through a number of events that will take place while incarcerated. You will learn which pitfalls to avoid and which opportunities to engage in. As you enter prison life, it will give you time to reflect on all past decisions made and to analyze and redirect your life's course. This book prepares you for the reality of prison, dispelling the myths or other noteworthy Hollywood urban legends.

Within Margaret Kohut's book, *When You Have to go to Prison: A Complete Guide for You and Your Family,* you will develop an understanding of the criminal justice system. Fortunately for you, this isn't a death sentence. You are in a state prison facility, and you have the opportunity to change law-breaking behavior and develop good characteristics and insight that will keep you out of future imprisonment. The key to surviving prison life is held within your attitude, adjusting to your environment and following the rules of the facility. This book warns you of the pitfalls to avoid, such as gang activity, sexual violence, contraband, drug trafficking, and "jailhouse lawyers."

Adapting to prison life will be a challenge. Your freedom is revoked, except for what little liberty is given within the prison walls. Habits you have grown accustomed to will cease — especially if they are seen as a security risk. You will be monitored 24 hours a day. Family visits will be limited, personal property is minimal, and privacy is relinquished. You will experience various levels of emotions, from fear to anger to restlessness. There are a cultural array of races, socioeconomic classes, and ethnic groups of individuals that will share in your personal space. This book will teach you how to manage your emotions while in a controlled setting; if not, you will soon learn there are great consequences — including an extension of prison time. Closely follow the fictional life of Tom in this book; he depicts a realistic example of the situations you may encounter during your time in prison and how to appropriately respond.

Kohut helps to steer your focus toward self-improvement and rehabilitation while you are in prison. Your family, health, spiritual life, and educational/vocational goals should be the primary focal points during your incarceration. Visualize what you want to accomplish, and start on these goals from day one. Challenge yourself while in prison to develop moral values, integrity, and accountability, and to act as a citizen worthy of parole. Kohut's book offers great advice on how to increase your chances of parole and positively influence your probability for an early release. It also offers great advice on how to maintain a good relationship with loved ones.

Guidance is provided for a smooth, healthy transition through the prison system back into American society. Absorb these tips to enhance your success and survival in prison. There is a great life outside the prison walls awaiting you.

Tina Bryant

*Licensed Independent Social Worker, Montana*

# Introduction

---

"Freedom to come and go as I please is exactly what I don't have, and maybe what I'll never have again."

*— The Journal of Augustus Hill, from the HBO television series by Tom Fontana*

---

If you are a first offender bound for prison, you may feel very much like Augustus Hill. You may recognize the name from the HBO drama "Oz," which is based on what life is like behind bars. The television series, created by Tom Fontana, centered on Emerald City, an experimental unit housed in Oswald State Correctional Facility that was designed to help prisoners rehabilitate themselves in a suitable environment. However, Em City instead became a breeding ground for rape, corruption, gang violence, double-dealing, murder, and drugs. The creators of "Oz" released a book called *The Journal of Augustus Hill* based on the fictitious narrator of the goings-on inside Em City. Neither the series nor the book paints a pleasant way of life inside prison walls, yet it still manages to capture moments of true caring among inmates and staff members, heroic ideas and deeds, and hope instead of despair.

Maybe it is finally sinking in that you really are headed for prison. There are no "get out of jail free" cards to save you; this is as real as it gets. If you are reading this book, you probably do not know much about the reality of prison life. What you see on television about what it is like to live in prison 24 hours a day may be interesting, and sometimes humorous, but very rarely is it accurate. Hollywood focuses on entertainment; this book is about real life in prison.

According to Michael Santos, a federal inmate who writes books and blogs about prison life and criminology, about 13.5 million Americans do time in some sort of incarceration every year. About 95 percent of these inmates go back to their communities after serving their sentences. Santos is serving a 45-year prison term for drug-related crimes and hopes to be released in 2013. At the time of his arrest, he was 23 years old. You and millions of other Americans are facing what many fear the most: a total lack of freedom.

In prison, you lose everything except some of the basic rights guaranteed to you by the U.S. Constitution. You are told when to wake up, when to go to sleep, when to eat, what to wear, what you may possess on your person or in your cell, what you cannot possess, where you must go, and where you cannot go. We do not really appreciate these forms of freedom until we lose them. Comfort, your personal identity, and privacy are practically non-existent in prison. Your basic needs will be met, but your desires most likely will not be met if they pose some kind of security risk. For example, in your home you can go to your kitchen and carve an apple with a paring knife. In prison, possession of a knife is a serious disciplinary offense.

We give up our freedom for many reasons, some ridiculous: A 37-year-old man in St. Paul, Minnesota, was arrested and charged with second-degree burglary for stealing eight piggy banks from a friend's house that contained only $2,700. At the time, he was on parole for first-degree burglary; his parole will be revoked, and he will return to prison to serve out his first sentence and then serve whatever sentence the court imposes upon him for the piggy bank heist. After escaping two first-degree murder charges a decade ago, O.J. Simpson will spend many years in prison — perhaps the rest of his life — for his part in a 2007 armed robbery in Las Vegas. In court, Simpson cited the reason for the robbery as an attempt get some of his sports memorabilia back from a person he believed to have acquired it. Was either of these crimes worth the consequences? A pervasive belief among criminals is that they will not be caught; if this were true, prison overcrowding in America would not be the serious problem that it is today.

I have worked within the civilian and military criminal justice system in some way for most of my adult life, beginning as a courtroom bailiff in the late 1970s. As a fugitive recovery agent ("bounty hunter"), corrections officer, and then in the U.S. Air Force as a therapist for civilian and military personnel who had committed crimes, my experiences more than convinced me that prison is not a good place to be. I also worked with family members of inmates and saw first-hand how difficult it is to maintain family bonds when a parent, child, or sibling is incarcerated. Now that I have retired to full-time writing, the torch has been passed to my beloved husband, Dr. Tristan Kohut, a physician with the Montana State Prison. It is to him I owe thanks for clarification of the many medical challenges that happen on the inside and the helplessness often felt by family members of ill or injured inmates.

Regardless of the reason for your incarceration, this book is meant to help you more quickly understand what life in prison is like; how to prepare yourself and your family for your time in prison; how to maintain important bonds with your spouse, partner, extended family, and children; and how to serve your time by putting it to good use. Staying out of trouble is a major "plus" when you meet with the parole board; this book will tell you how you can have a clean disciplinary file. If you have questions about how to maintain a close, healthy relationship with your children and/or partner, hopefully your questions will be answered here. Many inmates, family members, and prison staff members were interviewed for this book; it was my intention to speak with as many "real" people as possible rather that merely relying on existing research material. I want you and your family to have the most realistic information possible, and only people who are living or working in prison and their loved ones can truly give you the best, most accurate information about preparing for the prison experience. Many of these people are named and quoted directly; others were combined into a single case study to avoid confusion and conflicting information.

If you come across a term that is not fully explained or that you do not understand, you will find glossaries of legal terms and prison slang in appendices A and B. These terms relate to crimes for which you were convicted and defenses to those crimes that could form a basis for an appeal or a motion for a new trial if you pursue that route. It is most important that you understand these terms not only for yourself, but also so you can explain them to your family members.

By the time you finish this book, you will have gained a great deal of knowledge about preparing yourself and your family for your incarceration and what really happens in prison. Forget the Hollywood images; in this book, you will discover the truth.

# 1 Getting Accustomed to the Reality of Going to Prison

"Nobody really thinks they'll go to prison. We all think that either we will not even get caught, or that we'll just get probation or something. So when I did the crime, I didn't even think about prison. I can see a few months in the county jail, but the judge threw ten years at me, and for what? Just because I had some priors for petty theft. It is that 'habitual criminal' thing, or something like that. So here I am, sitting around doing nothing in prison for the next ten (expletive) years. People like me don't get parole."

— *J.N., Inmate, Montana*

The judge bangs his gavel, and that is it: You are going to prison. You have spent a few months in the county jail awaiting trial, and now it is all over. This is your first offense, but because you committed a felony, and not a misdemeanor, you will be doing your time in prison rather than the county jail. Not only did you commit a felony crime, but because your sentence is more than a year, you must serve your time in prison. Never in your wildest dreams did you ever imagine that you would be arrested, booked into jail, and appear in court dressed in a jumpsuit with your hands and feet shackled. You may have been a law-abiding citizen for years, but suddenly your world came crashing down when you made one mistake — a big mistake. You will not be seeing home again for several years, at least.

You think back on the movies and television shows you have seen about prison: the gang violence, brutal corrections officers, getting raped, and ending up in "the hole" for getting into trouble. And forget about the comforts of home: no television, having to do everything you are told to do exactly when you are told to do it, and having no privacy at all. When these images seem so real, it would be easy for you to feel a great deal of hopelessness, fear, and despair. Perhaps you worry that you will not even survive prison life long enough to have a chance at an early parole.

Hopefully, reading this book will help you understand the real prison experience; it is not a nice place to live, but it is not the living hell that you may have seen in movies and on television. Like everything else in life, living in prison is what you make of it. To help you understand more about what is in store for you in prison, we will address one issue at a time so you will not feel so lost and afraid when you hear those metal gates slam behind you. If you have more questions about prison, do not hesitate to talk to the person who gave you this book. The more answers you have about getting ready to go to prison, the less fearful you will be.

## WHAT IS THE DIFFERENCE BETWEEN JAIL AND PRISON?

The term "jail" usually refers to a county or city jail where you are held after being booked before you see the judge on a motion to set bail. Or, if you are convicted of a misdemeanor and received a sentence no longer than one year, you will serve this time in jail. If you are convicted of a felony (a more serious crime) and sentenced to serve time longer than one year, you will be transferred to a state prison.

Prisons are not designed to be comfortable. Their purpose is to remove dangerous people from society and offer them opportunities for rehabilitation to prevent them from committing other crimes. Prison is not necessarily as bad as you may have heard. In many ways, your experience in prison largely depends upon you — specifically, your attitude and behavior while you are "inside."

Prison can be a tolerable experience, especially if you stay out of trouble's way and take advantage of all the opportunities that are available to you for your rehabilitation. For example, if you committed robbery because you were unable to find a job and could not read or write, there are learning opportunities available in prison. Many educational skills are available to you, including earning your General Equivalency Diploma (GED). When you are released from prison, you will be able to find a job because you will have the equivalent of a high school diploma. You are on your way to prison, so ask yourself this question: If you were not incarcerated, would you try to improve your educational and technical skills on your own? Would you kick the habit of drugs and alcohol? Receive treatment for a serious medical condition?

These are not "pretend" questions; they are real-life questions for you to consider.

# PRISON DEMOGRAPHICS

If you have ever considered statistics pertaining to the prison system, the following section explains statistics from the U.S. Department of Justice, Bureau of Justice Statistics:

- According to a 2005 census of U.S. prison facilities, there were 1,821 state and federal prisons in America.

- More prisons and jails are currently under construction.

- More than 2.3 million Americans were incarcerated at the time of publication, and this number continues to increase.

- According to the U.S. Department of Justice Bureau of Justice Statistics, many inmates are incarcerated for violent crimes against others, and drug offenses remain the nation's top offences.

## Crimes committed by male Americans

Approximately 94 percent of U.S. prisoners are male. In order, the following crimes resulted in prison sentences for male Americans:

1. Drug offenses
2. Murder
3. Robbery

4.   Public order offenses such as DUI and prostitution

5.   Assault

6.   Burglary

7.   Sexual assault (not including rape)

8.   Larceny

9.   Fraud

10.  Rape

11.  Auto theft

12.  Manslaughter

## Crimes committed by female Americans

In Silja Talvi's 2007 book *Women Behind Bars: The Crisis of Women in the U.S. Prison System*, it lists the following crimes committed by women that land them in prison:

1.   Drug and alcohol offenses

2.   Crimes that are related to obtaining money for drugs and alcohol like burglary and receiving stolen property

3.   Repeated arrests for prostitution

4.   Property-related crimes like forgery, shoplifting, burglary, and auto theft

5.   Domestic-related homicide

## Prison populations by race and age

These statistics were also taken from the U.S. Department of Justice Statistics, 2005. You will be living with and among these inmates, so it is best to prepare now to plan your strategy for living in a harmonious "live and let live" system to avoid problems between you and other inmates who are different from you in one or many ways.

- 44.1 percent of inmates are African American, including those of Jamaican and Haitian descent who commit crimes in the U.S.

- 35 percent of inmates are Caucasian.

- 19 percent of inmates are Hispanic.

- 1.9 percent of inmates are of another race, such as Native American, American Eskimo, or Asian.

- 33.1 percent are between 30 and 39 years old.

- 33 percent are between 20 and 29 years old.

- 27.6 percent are between 40 and 54 years old.

- 4.3 percent are 55 or older.

- 2.1 percent are 19 or younger.

## A BRIEF LOOK AT THE AMERICAN CRIMINAL JUSTICE SYSTEM

You already know that you will be sent to prison, so you are fairly knowledgeable about the criminal justice system. You may or may not understand exactly how you got in this position other than committing the crime for which you were convicted and sentenced to prison. Sometimes inmates feel that they were "railroaded" through the system and did not really understand it. All the legal words and terms, over-worked and rushed defense attorneys, and the plea bargaining process are confusing for anyone who does not actually work in the system. You will also need to help your partner and/or children understand the criminal justice system to answer their many questions about what you did, how you were taken through the system, and what happens after you are incarcerated. We will take a look at two topics: criminal law and criminal procedure. *Criminal law* refers to the crime(s) that you committed and why they are illegal; *criminal procedure* refers to how the justice system works in America for those who commit crimes. To make this more understandable for you, we will use a hypothetical case study that is based upon the experiences of actual prison inmates. We will also use some "check your understanding" (CYU) sections to make sure you are learning what you need to know about the criminal justice system. You will find the answers to each CYU in Appendix C of this book. Along the way, you will find special sidebars that answer frequently asked questions, or FAQs.

## TOM'S STORY:

Tom is a 32-year-old white male who is in prison for the first time. He has a wife of eight years and two children, ages 6 and 4. Tom has had a serious drinking problem for no less than 10 years. He has tried, on his own, to stop or at least control his drinking, but he always returns to excessive drinking. Tom has never received formal treatment for his alcohol abuse, and he has never participated in a recovery program such as Alcoholics Anonymous® or Rational Recovery®. Last year, Tom lost his job as a sales manager for a local retail store. He was continually late to work, was continually hung-over, and drank while on the job. He has not found other employment because he does not have good work-related references. His wife is employed as a retail sales clerk and has been supporting the family; she told Tom that if he did not stop drinking after his second DUI, she would divorce him. In the past, Tom was arrested twice for driving under the influence of alcohol (DUI) and received a suspended sentence each time. One rainy night, Tom was returning home from his favorite bar. He was intoxicated but felt that he was able to drive. On a curve in the road, Tom lost control of the car and veered into the oncoming lane. He hit another car head-on at 50 miles per hour. A 17-year-old girl was driving the oncoming car; she was seriously injured in the wreck and is now confined to a wheelchair for the rest of her life. Tom was arrested and charged with a DUI, third offense, and felony assault with a deadly weapon (his car). He was booked into the county jail and scheduled for arraignment the following morning before Judge Jones. Tom did not speak with police officers at this time. At his arraignment, Tom was represented by a public defender who advised him to plead not guilty to both charges and request a jury trial. Tom did so, and remained in jail since he could not pay his bond of $25,000. As his trial date approached, Tom's public defender met with the district attorney (DA) who would be prosecuting Tom's case. In a plea bargain, Tom agreed to serve four years in prison in exchange for his plea of guilty to DUI, third offense, and the assault charge was reduced to simple assault rather than assault with a deadly weapon. After his plea of guilty, Tom was convicted and sentenced to four years in prison on the third-offense DUI charge and was given an additional two years for the assault charge. Tom was transported to the state prison to serve his sentence.

## Check Your Understanding No. 1

1. True or False:   Criminal law determines what actions are, and are not, illegal.

2. True or False:   Criminal procedure determines how the justice system works for people who are accused of a crime.

We will stop here for now and pick up Tom's story as we continue this chapter. This is a good place to examine both criminal law and criminal procedure in Tom's case. If some of these issues apply to you, hopefully this discussion will help you understand how criminal law and criminal procedure worked in your own case. Consider these points:

- Driving under the influence of any drug, including alcohol, is a criminal offense. It is against the law in all 50 states. Yet, each state has the right to determine the punishment for DUI offenses. In Tom's state, his first and second DUIs resulted in probation because no one was injured and no property was destroyed. The courts gave Tom two chances to stop drinking, but he failed to do so. His state's criminal laws require jail time for a third DUI offense. Tom also injured another person very badly, causing the DA and the judge to agree upon a prison term for Tom's assault on the teenage girl. Both of these offenses are felonies in all states.

- Tom's case illustrates several workings of *criminal procedure:* (1) He was arrested, meaning he was in the custody of police officers and could not leave the scene, and (2) Tom was declared to be "indigent," meaning he had no money to hire an attorney to represent him. The judge ordered that the office of the public defender represent Tom at no charge.

## What are Miranda rights?

In 1966, the U.S. Supreme Court made an important decision in the case of *Miranda v. Arizona,* which changed our criminal procedures forever. The Court ruled that whenever a person is taken into police custody, before being questioned he or she must be informed of the Fifth Amendment right not to make any self-incriminating statements. As a result of the Miranda case, anyone in police custody who is arrested on suspicion of committing a crime must be told four things before being questioned:

- You have the right to remain silent.

- Anything you say can and will be used against you in a court of law.

- You have the right to an attorney.

- If you cannot afford an attorney, one will be appointed for you.

**IMPORTANT:**

Your Miranda rights do apply while you are in prison. If you are accused of a crime while in prison, such as an assault upon another inmate, all four of these rights "attach," meaning that they apply to you immediately. Some good advice: Whenever you are advised of your right to remain silent or not, do so. Never speak about an alleged crime until you have spoken with an attorney.

In Tom's case, he went through the criminal procedures, or stages, of any criminal case: (1) arrest; (2) booking into the county jail; (3) arraignment, where the judge can set bail, order a defendant to remain in custody, appoint an attorney, set a date for various types of pre-trial hearings, and set a trial date; (4) conviction; and (5) sentencing. Later in Tom's case we will discuss another stage of criminal procedure — the appeal, or motion for a new trial.

Although he had a right to do so, Tom did not waive any of his Miranda rights. You can agree to speak with police officers about your alleged crime without first speaking with an attorney, but this is not a smart thing to do. A police officer's job is to get you to voluntarily confess to the crime if you really are guilty. They must, however, be very careful not to coerce (force) you to confess; if a judge determines that a confession is coerced, it cannot be used against a defendant in trial. Tom did not speak with anyone about his alleged offense until a public defender was appointed to represent him.

## Check Your Understanding No. 2

1. True or False:    One of your Miranda rights is to have a speedy trial.

2. True or False:    In criminal law, a felony crime is more serious than a misdemeanor crime.

3. True or False:    An arraignment is part of criminal procedure.

4. True or False:    Your Miranda rights do not apply once you go to prison.

# PAY ATTENTION TO YOUR ATTITUDE AND BEHAVIOR DURING COURT PROCEEDINGS

Anyone can be arrested and charged with a crime, but this does not mean the person is guilty of the crime. If you are innocent of the crime you are charged with, you must carefully watch your attitude and behavior in court. Court hearings are times and places where you need to be on your very best behavior by showing respect to the judge, jury, and prosecuting attorney. If you are angry and hostile in your attitude or behavior, you will not create a good impression to those people who hold your future in their hands. If you are guilty, the same rules of attitude and behavior apply; by making a good impression in court, you might find that your sentence is not as harsh as it could have been.

## The Innocence Project

The Innocence Project, founded by attorneys Barry Scheck, and Peter Neufeld, exists to prove the innocence of convicted men and women who are in prison for crimes they did not commit.

Since it began in 1992, this organization has helped to free 250 inmates who were convicted of major crimes using DNA testing. Twenty-four percent of these crimes were convictions for murder, while others involved sexual assaults. You may recall the 2007 case of Calvin Tillman, who served 16 years for a murder he did not commit, as proved by DNA testing conducted by the Innocence Project. Because other inmates on death row were exonerated with The Innocence Project, many states no longer have the death penalty. If you wish to contact The Innocence Project, you can do so by visiting their Web site at **www.innocenceproject.org**. This site explains its history and how to contact them by e-mail, telephone, or regular mail.

Like any governmental agency, the criminal justice system makes mistakes; on some occasions, a defendant is mistakenly convicted and sentenced to prison for a crime he or she did not commit. A well-known legal proverb is that it is better for 100 guilty men go free than for one innocent man to be imprisoned. In America, our criminal justice system carries the "presumption of innocence," meaning that a person charged with a crime is considered to be innocent until he or she is proven in court to be guilty and then declared guilty by a jury or judge. Another legal proverb says that in prison, no one is guilty; "I was framed!" or "You got the wrong guy!" is often heard on the inside. While this is often untrue, in many cases the inmate is telling the truth.

Whether you are still involved in criminal justice proceedings that seem likely to result in prison time or are in prison as you read this, it is possible that you may not be guilty of the crime(s) with which you were charged and/or convicted and sentenced.

This is a matter for you and your attorney to argue to a court and a jury.

If you are currently in prison and your attorney has filed an appeal of your case or has filed a motion for a new trial, you will be in the courtroom once again. Here is some legal terminology you need to know:

- An *appeal* to a higher court means that you were convicted and imprisoned because the judge made a serious error in applying the law during your trial or plea bargain. An appeal is based only upon issues of law, not issues of fact; a higher court will re-try your case and may find you not guilty.

- A *motion for new trial* usually happens when new evidence is discovered that may clearly indicate that if a jury heard this evidence, you could be found not guilty.

- *Innocent* and *not guilty* are not the same things. A judge or jury will not find you *innocent* of the crime; they will find you *not guilty* of the crime, meaning that the prosecution did not meet its burden of proof. The burden, in a criminal proceeding, is proof beyond a reasonable doubt.

We can use Tom's case as an example of this issue. Tom was guilty of his crimes; the only issue for the judge to decide was his sentence. If Tom was rude, belligerent, and physically aggressive, his judge would view him as a person who showed no remorse for his crimes and thereby deserving of a longer sentence in order to punish him, keep him off the street, and give him more time in prison to truly rehabilitate himself. On the other hand, if Tom was polite, remorseful, and cooperative with the court, he could receive a lighter sentence because he seemed a better candidate for rehabilitation in prison.

In summary, just mind your manners in court whether you are guilty or not. Appear in court clean and well-groomed. Address the judge and prosecutor as "sir" or "ma'am." Never let your temper get the best of you, no matter what. Remember, everything you say or do in a trial court or another type of court appearance creates a permanent impression upon those who will decide your fate. You cannot un-ring a bell.

## THE ROLE OF YOUR ATTORNEY AND THE PROSECUTOR

Whether you are still in the process of trial, appealing your case, or requesting a new trial, the prosecutor and your attorney are two people that you really need to show respect, so be sure to watch your attitude and behavior with them. They are serious people with serious jobs to do.

### *Your lawyer*

It is your lawyer's role to represent you during all legal matters in your case at all levels. If you are in prison and appealing your case, the law allows for an attorney to be appointed for you for only one appeal. From that point on, you must pay for a lawyer's services. Your lawyer works for you. He or she is your advocate in all aspects of your case regardless of whether you are guilty or not. Every lawyer takes an oath to "vigorously represent the client within the bounds of the law." It is your lawyer's task to make sure that you get a fair trial, with special emphasis on the prosecutor's burden of proof, which is beyond a reasonable doubt. If the prosecutor fails to meet this burden, the jury must find you not guilty since your guilt was not proven in court.

Your lawyer's job is to make sure your side is represented well in trial court or in an appeal, if you are convicted and sent to prison. Before you go to prison, your lawyer should obtain a transcript of your trial from the court reporter. You will need this if you appeal your case or make a motion for a new trial. Usually the same lawyer who represented you in your trial is the same lawyer who will represent you in at least one appeal or a motion for a new trial, but this is not always the case. *Before* you go to prison, make sure that your lawyer has obtained, or is in the process of obtaining, all legal documents and transcripts that you will need in future proceedings. Another legal term for you to consider is "post-conviction relief."

*Post-conviction relief* refers to all legal proceedings that occur after you are convicted. This includes appeals, motions for new trial, requests to be incarcerated in a prison close to your family, and anything that the law might interpret as cruel and unusual punishment that is prohibited by the U.S. Constitution.

The criminal justice system has definite rules; it has been compared to a football game with rules, procedures, and penalties — and both the defense and the prosecution want to win the game. Your lawyer's duty is to make absolutely certain that the prosecutor, who represents the people of your state, plays by the rules. This is the essence of your right to have a fair trial. Even if you are guilty, that right to a fair trial still must be enforced; you are not guilty until a judge or a jury says you are.

## Check Your Understanding No. 3

1. True or False:   "Jail" and "prison" are the same thing.

2. True or False:   In the case study, Tom committed a felony.

3. True or False:   Once you are in prison, you no longer need a lawyer.

4. True or False:   Only the facts of your case are important; your attitude and behavior in court play no part in your court proceedings.

## *The prosecutor*

The prosecutor, also called the district attorney or county attorney, is not your friend. He or she represents the people of your state and is duty-bound to do everything possible to make certain that you have a fair trial and are convicted and sentenced as appropriate for your crime. Before your trial — and even after you are sent to prison — never speak with a prosecutor or an investigator from the prosecutor's office without your attorney by your side. It is your attorney's job to object to any or all questions you are asked that violate your constitutional rights and advise you not to respond to these questions. Pay attention and do what your lawyer advises whether you are awaiting trial or have already been sentenced to prison.

## A LEGAL VOCABULARY LESSON

During legal proceedings, you will hear the attorneys refer to the trial judge as "Your Honor," "Judge," or "the Court." Example: "We request that the Court rule on our motion for a new trial." You will also hear the attorneys referred to as "Counsel" or "Counselor." Example: "I object to the defense counsel's question, Your Honor."

# PRE-SENTENCE INVESTIGATIONS: HOW THEY CAN HURT YOU AND HELP YOU

After you are convicted of a crime, the judge usually orders a pre-sentence investigation (PSI) no matter whether a sentence is decided by the judge or the jury; this may vary from state to state. PSIs are usually done by probation or parole officers and contain a "snapshot" of your background to help the person or people decide what sentence is appropriate for you as an individual. To give you an example of how a PSI can both hurt you and help you, let us return to Tom's case:

Before Tom's sentencing hearing, the judge ordered a probation officer to prepare a PSI on Tom's background and history of prior offenses. After speaking with Tom on several occasions, the probation officer also spoke with his prior employer, his wife, his victim (the teenage girl), and two of his friends. The PSI contained the following information that could hurt Tom as the judge considers his sentence:

- Tom has two prior convictions for DUI.

- Tom has never participated in treatment for his alcohol problem.

- Tom was fired from his job due to excessive alcohol use.

- Tom's closest friends also abuse alcohol in bars.

- The teenager who Tom hit while driving drunk will never walk again.

- The teenager's family has only limited insurance; they are unable to pay for the total cost of her medical care.

- The teenager wrote a *victim impact statement* for the judge saying that she has become extremely depressed since Tom injured her, has thought of suicide several times, and once had to be admitted to a psychiatric hospital. She will need long-term psychiatric care.

- Tom's wife stated that she does not want him back in their home and that she may divorce him because of his drinking.

The following is information contained in Tom's PSI that may help him:

- Tom has skills as a salesman that could help him get a job when he is released from prison.

- Tom's former boss stated that Tom was good at his job, and he would not have been fired if he had not had a serious drinking problem.

- Tom did not have disciplinary actions while awaiting trial in the county jail.

- Tom's behavior and attitude have been appropriate during all his court appearances.

- Tom prepared a statement for the court expressing remorse for his actions; he promised to contribute a part of his income during and after prison to make restitution to his victim to help the family pay medical bills.

- Tom has no history of gang membership or any kind of violence.

- Tom has no drug history other than excessive alcohol abuse.

As you can see, a PSI contains both positive and negative elements of a person's life, which any person will have. The difference between Tom and most others is that Tom committed a serious criminal offense that left a young girl paralyzed for life.

## LET'S MAKE A DEAL: PLEA BARGAINS AND SENTENCING

The official definition of a plea bargain, according to historian Joel Samaha, is "the process of negotiating an agreement out of court among the defendant, the prosecutor, and the judge as to an appropriate plea and sentence in a criminal case. Two advantages of plea bargains are that they circumvent the trial process and dramatically reduce the time usually required for the resolution of such a case."

## *Who Benefits in Plea Bargains?*

Plea bargains are good for numerous reasons. Keep in mind that in all 50 states and U.S. territories, hundreds of crimes are committed each day and in every city. As things stand, our justice system cannot possibly handle the load of all these cases in a timely manner, although our Constitution guarantees every criminal defendant the right to a speedy trial. But since the Constitution and its Bill of Rights were written soon after the 1776 revolution, the founding fathers could not possibly have imagined how much America would grow in both land and population. It makes sense to find that as our population and size grew, so did our crime level. Today, America leads the world in the number of criminal charges that are filed each year, including murder charges. There are many reasons for this — perhaps this is something you might follow through in learning about when you are in prison. But for our purposes in this book, it is enough for you to know that our courts are extremely clogged with the sheer number of criminal defendants that come before judges and juries every day. If not for plea bargains, judges and district attorneys would have a much more crowded calendar, and defendants who cannot afford bail would remain in jail even though they might not be guilty of the crime for which they were charged.

Consider this example: You are the owner of a chainsaw that a defendant stole from your home during the night. The defendant was charged with the felony of first-degree burglary and was then released on bail of $10,000. The case is scheduled to go to court in about eight months. You need that chainsaw to perform your work as a carpenter. But until the trial and jury's verdict, the chainsaw is considered to be evidence in the case and must remain in police custody. Your attorney tries to have the trial moved forward to no avail, and you must pay all your court costs and attorney's fees. In breaking down this scenario, we find that (1) you cannot work because a valuable piece of property was stolen from you; (2) the trial judge's and DA's calendars are jam-packed; (3) your attorney charges $200 per hour, including telephone calls about the case; and (4) the person accused of stealing your chainsaw is out on bail.

The defendant has two other felony charges against him in other cases. If he is convicted in each trial, he automatically becomes eligible for the "three strikes and you're out" sentence of life in prison without parole. The district attorney tells your attorney that the people will accept the defendant's plea to a lower offense of misdemeanor breaking and entering. When the judge accepts the plea bargain, several things happen: (1) The defendant is no longer subject to life without parole; (2) the calendar of the judge and district attorney becomes lighter; and (3) you get your chainsaw back and save money on your attorney fees.

If our courts are clogged, it follows naturally that our prisons are even more clogged; in fact, they are overly full. In his book *Behind a Convict's Eyes,* inmate K.C. Carceral wrote of his belief that prison overcrowding explains why vital services within the prison — such as kitchens, medical, and treatment programs — are either unavailable or have experienced huge budget cuts. Crowded prisons make it difficult for many of the programs and services to operate well. In the past few decades, Americans have had to make some compromises to cope with court and prison overcrowding. One of those compromises is plea bargaining.

If you are involved in a criminal case that will result in prison, as in Tom's case, and you are offered a plea bargain through your attorney, look at the situation this way: Most criminal defendants do not have any money to hire a private attorney, unless the case involves a wealthy client such as O.J. Simpson. It is well known that Simpson hired the best — very expensive — lawyers to represent him: Johnnie Cochran, Barry Scheck, Robert Shapiro, and F. Lee Bailey. The reason these lawyers were so expensive was because of their enormous skill in raising reasonable doubt for the jurors about their clients' guilt. They did their jobs magnificently, and the results are well known, whether you agree with the jury's "not guilty" verdict or not.

Many criminal defendants do not have the means to hire private attorneys and must rely upon the public defender's (PD) office. Do not misunderstand: PDs are competent trial lawyers in every way, but they are public servants just like prosecutors. They do not make a great deal of money, and they have hundreds of cases open at any given time. Being realistic, they have little time to represent their clients in a lengthy court trial. After the Simpson trial, many members of the public wondered if there was a criminal justice system for the rich and famous and another one for the poor and middle-class. We cannot dwell on criminal philosophy in this book, but you and your family must face the reality that your case may not come to trial for many months, and that if you are sent to prison, you will find overcrowding in virtually every prison. One of the reasons our system uses plea bargains is to reduce the number of cases going to trial and to reduce the number of convicted defendants who go to prison. Tom, our example inmate, received probation for his first two DUI convictions.

Contrary to some conflicting opinions, it does not appear that America has "gotten soft on crime." It is more correct to say that, without plea bargains, we would need billions of dollars to hire more judges, PDs, and prosecutors; pay more jurors; build more prisons that are required to provide food, clothing, education, treatment programs, and medical care; buy more exercise equipment for inmates; and hire more parole officers, medical staff, corrections officers, teachers, and mental health counselors. This is only a short list of the upkeep needed in jails and prisons. We must not forget about electricity, water, and sanitation costs. American taxpayers pay these bills. When you go to prison, you pay for nothing except what you buy at the canteen.

When you accept a plea bargain either before your trial or due to an offense committed in prison, you are agreeing to forgo a verdict and plead guilty to a lesser offense, thereby receiving a shorter sentence than you were previously facing. In Tom's case, he pled guilty to DUI. He accepted a plea bargain on the advice of his attorney to reduce his assault with a deadly weapon charge to simple assault, a less serious crime, if the prosecutor recommended that the judge reduce his sentence on this charge. A defense attorney knows that the prosecutors and courts are overburdened and will make a request for a defendant to plead guilty to a lesser crime in return for less prison time.

It is very important for you to remember that while you are in prison, you can still commit crimes like assault, drug trafficking, and even murder, and be fully prosecuted for those crimes and extend your time in prison; you can even receive the death penalty for crimes committed in prison. It is in your best interest to listen carefully when your attorney brings you an offer of a plea bargain, but you always have the final say as to whether you will accept it or not.

# UNDERSTANDING THE GOALS OF INCARCERATION

Before you go to prison, you and your family should understand why you are about to become incarcerated. Traditionally, the goals of incarceration are:

- Removing dangerous people from society

- Rehabilitation of criminals

- Retaliation/revenge

We will look at these goals one at a time to help you understand and explain to your family why a judge or jury believed that prison time was the answer in your case.

## *Removing dangerous people from society*

The entire nation, and perhaps the entire civilized world, was horrified by the crimes of Jeffrey Dahmer. Between 1987 and 1991, Dahmer drugged, killed, and ate 17 young men in Milwaukee, Wisconsin. Although he appeared to express sincere remorse for his crimes, Dahmer was considered to be too dangerous to ever live among society again. He was sentenced to life in prison without parole (a fellow prison inmate killed Dahmer in November 1994). Dahmer was not alone; our prisons are full with those convicted for terrible crimes from serial murder to rape to rampant drug trafficking. The theory here is that there are some people, like

41

Dahmer and many others, who are just too criminally minded to live outside prison. Society must be protected from them. If you are going to prison, then a judge or jury has decided that you must first be removed from society for some length of time until it is safe for you to live in society again as a law-abiding citizen who presents no threat to others. This does not only include crimes of violence. People have a right to feel safe in their homes without someone stealing their belongings, forging their checks, selling drugs, or yanking their cars out of their garages. This is why crimes of violence, even *negligent violence* as in Tom's case, result in longer sentences than non-violent crimes. Both are wrong, but the degree of "wrongness" is higher in crimes that result in bodily harm to another person.

## *Rehabilitation of prisoners*

- FBI crime reports and statistics regarding prison inmates clearly suggest that the majority of prisoners in the U.S. have not finished high school and have no technical job-related skills. While you are preparing yourself to go to prison, give some serious thought about what kind of educational skills you need to obtain during your incarceration. When you meet the parole board, you will be able to show that you have used your time in prison well by obtaining job skills through your own self-discipline. Also think about whether you need to receive drug or alcohol treatment in prison, especially if your crime was drug-related, alcohol-related, or a sexual offense. If you have the means to get a job to support yourself and your family when you are released, this will decrease your odds of committing another crime.

In addition to educational programs, you will find that prisons also offer special classes to help change your behavior, such as anger and stress management. These programs are designed so you will no longer be a danger to society. For example, if you are going to prison for domestic violence, you can use your time wisely by learning how to manage problems in your relationships without harming your partner. In a victim empathy program, you will learn the negative impact that your actions had on the victim of your crime.

Many people who are going to prison for the first time wonder whether there are some people who will never feel remorse for their crimes and do not wish to make good use of rehabilitation programs. The answer is "yes," and you are going to meet them. These inmates are usually serving very long sentences — even life without parole — because they committed many violent crimes. They are called "dangerous habitual offenders." In these cases, the law presumes that these inmates are not capable of being rehabilitated and must be permanently separated from society. While in prison, these inmates will continue their violence and other illegal behaviors and often must be housed in a maximum-security unit for the safety of other inmates and the prison staff. It is very important that you stay away from these inmates; association with them will most likely cause you to be labeled a "troublemaker" as well, and this will greatly diminish your chances of parole.

## Programs commonly available in prison

To receive state or federal funding, prisons must offer, at least, the following programs. Some inmates, such as those on death row, are not strictly required to attend any of these programs. However, if an inmate hopes to make a good impression on a parole board, he or she will play it smart and attend everything offered.

1.  Reading/writing

2.  High school equivalency (GED)

3.  Drug/alcohol recovery

4.  Anger management

5.  Conflict management

6.  Victim empathy

7.  Impulse control

8.  Auto mechanics

9.  Welding

10. Computer skills

11. Parenting skills

## *Retaliation/revenge*

While you are preparing to go to prison, think about exactly why you will soon become incarcerated. The purposes of sending an offender to prison are often the subject of heated debates. The most common goals of incarceration are those listed in this section, including retaliation/revenge. Since you committed a crime against the laws of society, we the people of this society have a right to punish you for that crime by taking away your freedom. The Eighth Amendment of the U.S. Constitution protects you from "cruel and unusual punishment," including failure to provide you with food, clothing, shelter, and medical care. Society believes that when a person's freedom is taken away for any reason, society members are then responsible to ensure all their basic needs are met. Although this costs the American taxpayers billions of dollars every year, this is the price we must pay to be a civilized society with laws and morals.

In England, Scotland, Ireland, and other countries before reforms were made in the 20th century, punishment for crimes was swift, severe, and harsh, and there were no courts for appeals. For example, the punishment for stealing was for the thief to have his or her hand cut off. Repeat offenders were simply hanged. Nathaniel Hawthorne's book about colonial America, *The Scarlet Letter*, is about female adultery, which was, at the time, still a crime for women. The punishment was often to have the letter "A" branded on their foreheads or permanently placed on their clothing so everyone who saw them knew that they were unfaithful to their husbands. Probably the worst punishment began during the 12th century in Britain: the practice of hanging, drawing and quartering for the crime of murder or rebellion against the King or Queen. In this case, a man was hung by the neck until he was almost dead, then cut down and had his arms and legs cut off. Finally, he was stabbed in the abdomen and all of his intestines were drawn out, then thrown into a fire – all while he was still alive. Even today in some Arabic countries that are ruled by the Islamic religion, women who commit adultery are subject to "honor killing" by her husband or father. Those in Middle Eastern cultures who commit serious crimes are subject to immediate execution by beheading.

Keep in mind that in the United States, you are protected by the Eighth Amendment to the U.S. Constitution against "cruel and unusual punishment." This specifically includes torture, such as cutting off a criminal's limbs or the horrific punishments described earlier. A convicted inmate also cannot have his or her United States citizenship revoked. Still, the Supreme Court has ruled that the death penalty is *not necessarily* cruel and unusual punishment, depending upon how it is carried out.

There are many other examples of cruel and unusual punishment in Supreme Court case law. If you wish to know more about the Eighth Amendment and how it protects inmates, your prison law library is available to you for such research.

## Check Your Understanding No. 4

Review the chapter and make sure you understand these terms:

1. Jail
2. Prison
3. Felony
4. Misdemeanor
5. Goals of incarceration
6. Plea bargain
7. Miranda rights
8. Appeal
9. Public defender
10. Motion for new trial
11. Pre-sentence investigation (PSI)
12. Criminal procedure
13. Criminal law
14. Burden of proof
15. Prison overcrowding

# REVENGE VS. PUNISHMENT FOR CRIMES

Perhaps you have heard the saying, "The punishment must fit the crime." Very early in U.S. history, our Supreme Court forbade exceedingly cruel punishments that were only revenge-based. You are going to prison to be removed from society while you are being rehabilitated, and also to punish you for your crime by denying you your freedom to come and go as you please. More serious crimes, especially those that involve violence, mean a longer sentence before an inmate is eligible for parole. Severe crimes of violence can result in being sentenced to life without parole or the death penalty in states that allow it.

The idea behind the punishment element of incarceration is that serving a long sentence punishes you harshly enough, thus making you think twice before you commit another crime. This is also known as "deterrence." One of the odd things about the American criminal justice system is that we are one of only a few countries that still allow the death penalty as discussed in the last section. This is clearly revenge, or "a life for a life" according to the Christian Bible (Old Testament). It also succeeds in permanently removing the worst, most violent offenders from society. But life sentences without parole and the death penalty serve the same purpose. The harsh sentences obviously do not focus on rehabilitation. A "lifer" has no need to improve his education skills or have remorse for his crime because he knows he will never be paroled.

Before we leave this chapter, keep in mind that while you are in prison, you may not get everything you want, such as having visitors, watching television, and exercising in the recreation area.

Perhaps this is a part of your punishment for committing a crime that will keep you from offending again in the future. However, you will get everything you really need. Americans have no need for cruel and unusual punishment. The U.S. government, elected by the people, believes the loss of freedom is the most severe punishment of all. The smartest thing you can do is to make sure that you lose your freedom only once.

# CHAPTER 2

# What to Know Before You Go

Reading this book will give you a head start on knowing the details about prison life that many first-time inmates have to find out slowly as they adjust to serving time. By the time you arrive and get settled in, you will already know valuable information such as the jobs of prison staff members, the difference in the levels of security, what you can and cannot bring with you to prison or ever have in your possession, how to use the prison commissary, how inmates are classified, and "who's who" among inmates. This will make your entry into prison much less confusing and fearful.

We will also examine some common myths and stereotypes about prison that generally come from television and movies. In this book, you will find the truth, not Hollywood's entertaining yet false impressions of what it is like to live and work inside.

No matter where you will be serving your time, living with many people in a relatively small space can create a great deal of tension. In jail, the population shifts continuously since only people awaiting trial or serving less than a year are confined to jail. But in prison, the population remains much more stable because the inmates are serving longer sentences — some for the rest of their lives. We have already discussed the serious issue of overcrowding in prisons and the many problems this causes; this is an issue you should be aware of before you go to prison and emotionally prepare yourself to cope with it.

# COMMUNITIES WITHIN COMMUNITIES

A prison is a community that is set apart from the communities in cities where people live and work every day. For example, the Oklahoma State Prison is located in McAlester, Oklahoma. Think of McAlester as a large community, and the prison as being a smaller community within the larger community. Cities and prisons have many things in common, as well as other aspects that make them extremely different from one another.

Cities and prisons have the following things in common:

- Both have officials who are in charge of running them. In a city, that official is the mayor. In prison, it is the *warden*.

- Both have rules, or laws, that residents must follow or risk disciplinary actions.

- Not everyone gets along. Sometimes there is tension among the residents of both cities and prisons.

- Both offer educational and social skills programs to residents.

- Both have language terms that are unique to them, called an "argot." For example, in a big city the term "busting loose" means going out on the town and having a great time. In prison, this is a term for escape.

## WHAT IS A PENITENTIARY?

This is merely another word for prison that began in the 1700s in the colonial days of early America. Some religious groups believed that through intense study of the Bible, inmates would become "penitent" (remorseful) and change their law-breaking behavior.

Cities and prisons have the following differences:

- People live in various cities because they choose to. They like the location, job opportunities, and other key factors about the city. People live in prison because they are forced to do so by a court of law for having committed a serious crime.

- People who live in a city can leave and change locations any time they want. Prison inmates cannot leave the prison until they are either granted parole or serve their entire sentence.

- The people of a city elect the mayor; a prison warden is appointed or hired by the state's Department of Corrections.

Now that you understand how cities and prisons have similarities and differences, try to think of prison as a community within a community. As you prepare to go to prison, keep in mind that the same things happen in prison that happen in the city surrounding the prison. People still break rules, harm each other, sell drugs, commit sex offenses, and steal from each other. On the other hand, people in prison do many acts of kindness for others, practice their religion, take a keen interest in their families, and provide good role models for others. Your own experience in prison will be what you chose to make of it, for better or worse.

# WHO'S WHO IN PRISON

Each prison staff member has a specific job. Once you understand who performs what job, you will know who to call if you need help, if you would like to volunteer to help others, with whom to file a grievance against another inmate or a staff member, and who to stay away from.

## The state's department of corrections (DOC)

The department of corrections is the government agency responsible for building and maintaining the state's prisons and providing for all inmates' needs from food to medical care to clothing. The DOC also sets policy and procedures for individual staff members.

## The prison warden and his/her deputy warden

The warden and deputy warden govern the day-to-day administration of the prison. Everything that happens inside the prison is their responsibility. Wardens usually have college degrees in penology (the study of prisons) or criminal justice. Many prison and deputy wardens work their way up through the ranks from being corrections officers. Inside the prison, the warden is the go-to person for every aspect of prison life and the prison's administration. Sometimes inmates with especially good behavior records and who are nearing their release date work in the warden's or deputy warden's office just like a 9-to-5 job on the outside. It is not a good idea to do things that put you on the bad side of the warden or deputy warden; these people have great influence with the parole board.

## The classification team

The classification team is also called Assessment and Evaluation, or A&E. They are the staff members — usually social workers, psychologists, or administrative staff members — who assign inmates to custody and security levels based on their offense histories, degree of dangerousness to others, and possible risk of escape. When you arrive in prison, you will be assigned to minimum, medium, or maximum custody and security levels. Depending upon your crime, your attitude about being in prison, the possibility that you may harm other inmates or staff, and information about your intention to escape from prison, the classification team will decide where you should be housed within the prison. We can use Tom's case as an example of this system.

### How classification works:

When Tom first arrived at the state prison, he met with the A&E classification team while he was still in administrative "hold," or segregation, like all inmates who are new to the prison. In deciding which custody and security level was in Tom's best interests and for the safety of staff and other inmates, the team considered the following information:

- This is the first time Tom has been in prison.

- Tom has a previous criminal history of two DUIs.

- Tom has no disciplinary history while in jail.

- Tom does not appear to be an escape risk.

- Tom has never been a gang member.

- Tom has no history of being a sexual predator.

- Tom was pleasant and cooperative with the A&E team.

- Tom's crime resulted in harm to a teenage girl; this could put him in danger from other inmates.

- Tom has no history of drug use other than alcohol but most likely has anger and depression issues, which are common with alcohol dependence.

The team decided that Tom should be housed in the medium security and custody unit because of his two previous offenses and the assault of the teenage victim. If Tom maintained good behavior in medium custody, avoided impulsive actions, did not associate with "troublemaker" inmates, and accepted total responsibility for his crime and his rehabilitation, he could eventually be transferred to minimum security and custody housing.

"I never been locked up before. Jail, yeah, but not prison. There's a big difference. I didn't know who did what and how to get along. This old guy who'd been inside for ten years kind of took me under his wing and taught me the ropes. It's easy to say and do the wrong thing in prison that could get you locked in segregation or get you killed."

— *G.B., Inmate, Montana State Prison*

Another aspect of classification is determining which prison programs an inmate needs to utilize in order to rehabilitate. In Tom's case, the team would recommend alcohol recovery counseling, stress management, employment counseling, and possibly family counseling if Tom's wife was willing to participate.

Looking at another example of how the classification process works, we can examine the history of another type of inmate who was admitted to maximum security:

- The inmate has been to prison before; both times he committed violent offenses.

- He is a solid member of the Aryan Brotherhood (AB), a white supremacy gang that advocates harm — or death — to all non-white inmates.

- The first time he was in prison, he was suspected of smuggling heroin into his unit from visitors who were also AB members, including his wife.

- Also during his first incarceration, this inmate was found with a knife in his possession during a search of his cell.

- He has no interest in rehabilitation programs of any kind.

During his incarceration, K.C. Carceral found that the lower the custody and security level, the more freedom and privileges an inmate has. He explains the difference between these:

**Custody levels** determine how an inmate gets along with other inmates and his or her behavior in prison.

**Security levels** determine what kind of risk, if any, an inmate poses to staff members or other inmates. Carceral makes a point of writing that in prison, an inmate's "rep" (reputation) is tremendously important. "A rep will either make you or break you in prison," he wrote. "The worst rep to have is a snitch." This is an example of why some inmates might be in maximum custody: not because he or she has done anything wrong, but because he or she has a rep of snitching to staff about the behavior of other inmates that break the rules of the prison. This puts the prisoner at risk from other inmates.

## Corrections officers (COs)

The American Correctional Association (**www.aca.org**) is comprised of about 350,000 people working in prisons today. Most of these people are corrections officers, once called guards. The most important jobs of these men and women are to maintain control over the prison's inmates and to keep general order in the prison to ensure that inmates follow the rules and do not harm other inmates or staff. These highly trained public servants usually bear the brunt of Hollywood's stereotyping. With a few exceptions, such as Tom Hanks in *The Green Mile*, COs are frequently portrayed as corrupt, brutal, and altogether bad guys. In the television series *Prison Break*, the good guys were the inmates and the COs were portrayed negatively. We will talk more about prison staff stereotypes later in this chapter. But since you are about to go to prison, or are new to prison, you and your family should understand that a well-trained, serious-minded CO may be all that stands between you and disaster if you are faced with a dangerous gang member, a snitch who will say anything to get out faster, or a medical emergency.

COs are employees of each state's DOC. They must go through an intensive training program much like the police academy but with a focus on special issues such as preventing gang violence, drug trafficking, security, and accounting for every inmate in the prison. Custody and control are the primary functions of COs.

Beginning on the day you arrive in prison, refer to all COs as "sir," "ma'am," "officer," or "CO (last name)." In some prisons, COs are called "boss." Regardless, speak to them with courtesy and respect, and that is how you will be treated. If your COs seem to be rather formal or distant with you, keep in mind three points:

- COs are not your enemies, but they are also not your friends. They are very serious about their jobs, as they must be to protect the public and maintain control over the prison. As long as you do what they tell you, when they tell you to do so, you will have no difficulties. If you are in some kind of difficulty, you can trust them to help you. But if you cause a problem, they will react quickly and with complete authority.

- In state prisons, COs are outnumbered by inmates in a 4 to 1 ratio. Since there are less of them than there are inmates, it is essential that they use their wits and training to keep safety and order within the prison. They have gear to subdue an unruly inmate, stop a gang fight, and end a riot. When one CO is threatened by an inmate, other COs will instantly come to his or her aid, and then it is the inmate who is outnumbered by a show of force that COs are not afraid to use when absolutely necessary.

---

"All human beings, regardless of who they are, where they come from, or what they have done should be treated with respect and dignity. COs should always perform their duties in a professional manner. If they are not capable of being positive role models, they should find employment elsewhere."

– *Corrections Officer,* **www.insideprison.com**

---

- The ACA requires that women as well as men have opportunities to become COs. They are as fully trained, physically and mentally, as men. Do not make the mistake of thinking that a female CO is "soft" on either male or female inmates and likely to avoid confrontations with inmates who are breaking the rules of the prison. These are some of the most assertive women you will ever meet; they have to be tough to do their job in a man's prison as well as a women's prison. Always speak to female COs with respect, watch your language, and never make sexual comments to them; this is an extremely serious offense that your parole board will make special note of since you are asking to be released back into a society full of women.

## Check Your Understanding No. 5

1. True or False:    A prison is like a small community within a city, a larger community.

2. True or False:    The classification team determines when you will be released from prison.

3. True or False:    Custody levels and security levels are the same thing.

4. True or False:    It is unlikely that you will ever meet the prison warden or deputy warden.

5. True or False:    The primary duties of corrections officers are custody and control.

## *The security chief (SC)*

The security chief is a high-status CO who has risen through the ranks and is ultimately in charge of all the COs and ensuring all prison policies pertaining to security issues are followed. Usually, at the end of each shift, the on-duty SC is briefed by the CO in charge of that shift about possible security risks and any errors that have been made in security procedures, so each CO can learn from these mistakes. We can use Tom's case as an example of the duties of the security chief.

About three months into his sentence, Tom suffered an acute attack of appendicitis. Since the prison physician does not perform surgery inside the prison, Tom needed to be transferred by a prison ambulance to a hospital in the local community for surgery. Because Tom is a medium-security inmate, prison policy was that he should be in leg and arm shackles during the transport. The medical team made Tom comfortable in the ambulance and the COs applied the necessary shackles. Two COs rode in the ambulance with Tom, along with a medical technician. As prison policy required, a "chase car" went in front of the ambulance with two armed COs on board. However, there was no chase car following in back of the ambulance; this was a violation of prison policy. The purpose of chase cars is to prevent an inmate's escape while being transported to and from any location outside the prison.

In addition, Tom was told that a member of the medical staff would transport him to the hospital within the hour. This too is a prison policy security violation; an inmate is never told when a transfer will happen, so as to prevent escape plans. Although Tom made no effort to escape, the security chief was informed of these two mistakes. He called a meeting of all the COs and medical personnel and reminded them that both front and rear chase cars were required, and that Tom should not have been told when he would be transferred. The SC praised the COs for keeping to the policy that requires at least one (sometimes two, for dangerous inmates) CO to remain with the inmate as long as he or she is in the hospital. Your rights as an inmate for protection from harm include: (1) food, clothing, and shelter; (2) protection against foreseeable attack from other inmates; (3) protection from predictable sexual abuse; and (4) protection against suicide. It is the security chief who is ultimately responsible for ensuring you receive these rights.

# YOUR MEDICAL TREATMENT IN PRISON

## *The medical staff*

- At least one physician, but sometimes two or three
- A physician's assistant
- Registered nurses (RNs)
- Nurse practitioners
- A psychiatrist
- A dentist
- Several medical technologists

---

"Mr. (inmate) came to see me complaining of intense pain from kidney stones. I had him give me a urine sample, which is the normal procedure. When the lab analyzed the sample, they found pieces of concrete in it. Mr. (inmate) was merely trying to obtain narcotic pain medicine."

— *Dr. T. K, Prison Physician*

---

In *Through a Convict's Eyes*, Carceral tells his story of medical care as an inmate; he is not complimentary of the American correctional medical system and calls it "third-world medical," meaning that it is no better, and often worse, than in very poor countries. He quotes an inmate as saying, "They treat dogs in the pound better than us." To be fair, Carceral also quotes a medical staff member who said, "I see guys go every now and then to the hospital; I wish my family could get years of free medical care."

The truth is that under the landmark Supreme Court case of *Estelle v. Gamble,* every inmate must receive adequate medical care either inside the prison or in the local community. This does not mean that you will get the type of medical care that you want, but you will receive the humane medical care that you need. Many inmates make the mistake of believing that because the state took away their freedom, they can have any type of medical care they wish — this is not true. When their wishes are not met, they complain that they are not receiving adequate care.

Quick-thinking and caring physicians, RNs, and other medical staff members have saved many lives. In fact, prison physicians are experts in correctional medicine or are actively working to obtain this level of skill to ensure that inmates are taken care of appropriately. Correctional medicine is different from non-prison medicine. For example, your physician will have more limited categories of medications available for you. Inmates are not allowed to be placed on waiting lists for organ transplants.

Most importantly, your physician must always keep security issues in mind when prescribing medications that can be abused or sold or doling out any type of assisted-walking devices — such as canes or crutches — that could be used as weapons. Any medical staff member who fails to meet standards of care is either put on administrative probation or fired. Prison medicine has come a long way in the past century; physicians must be able to treat such modern problems as "meth mouth," amputations among diabetic inmates, depression, and pain management, as well as care for terminally ill inmates.

The best thing you can do to prepare yourself to go to prison is to obtain every bit of medical information about yourself that you can lay your hands on. This information should include all major medical problems and injuries you are currently experiencing or have experienced in the past; dental records; psychiatric records; Veteran's Administration records; vaccines you have received; your sexual history as far as sexually transmitted diseases (including HIV or AIDS); a list of your medications; and medical test results such as blood work, X-rays, and gynecology results. When you are processing into the prison and in administrative segregation, medical staff members will review these records. You may receive tests for drug-related illnesses such as HIV, AIDS, or hepatitis and given vaccinations. Your classification team in A&E will include a thorough physical and gynecological exam. Female inmates also receive a pregnancy test.

In regards to your medical care while in prison, you are entitled to the following basic health rights: (1) sanitary and healthy living conditions; (2) medical attention for serious physical and psychiatric conditions; (3) any necessary medications; and (4) adequate treatment as prescribed by your physician. If you believe these rights have been violated, you also have the right to file a grievance or a lawsuit.

Some inmates come to prison with serious illnesses such as HIV/ AIDS, lung cancer, liver disease and/or brain and nerve damage caused by alcohol addiction, heart disease, and kidney disease.

Inmates are usually not eligible to receive high-cost surgeries for these conditions. The reason for this is not because the justice system sees criminals as "throw-away" people that no one cares about any longer but that these types of medical care are simply too expensive. Part of each American taxpayer's taxes goes to the state's DOC. This money goes toward the upkeep of our prison systems, including your medical care.

Having a serious or even terminal illness is not a guarantee that you will be released early from prison. In fact, it is very unlikely; inmates serving lengthy or life sentences tend to die in prison. While this may seem harsh, the medical staff will go out of their way to make a dying inmate comfortable, pain-free, and provide visits from friends, family, pastors, and counselors.

## The mental health team

- Psychiatrist
- Psychologists
- Counselors
- Professional therapists

When you arrive at the prison, you will have a complete mental examination to determine if you need — or have had — treatment for depression, anxiety, bipolar illness (manic depression), schizophrenia, impulse control disorders, substance abuse disorders, and personality disorders that affect how you think and behave. Another Hollywood stereotype is that mentally ill inmates receive no treatment and are allowed to put other inmates and staff at risk of harm. The truth is that your mental health needs will be fully treated while you are incarcerated. This can include drug/alcohol counseling as well as individual and family therapy to help make your return to society easier, which in turn will make you less likely to commit other crimes.

It is in your best interests to ensure your mental health needs are identified and treated; this is a subject of great interest to the parole boards. It is not legal for you to be forcibly given medication to keep you under control unless you are clearly a danger to yourself or others. Medications are given only when there is a clear need for them to help you treat your mental health condition(s).

## DO CORRECTIONS OFFICERS CARRY FIREARMS INSIDE THE PRISON?

No. This also is a security issue, strictly enforced by the security chief. COs know how easy it might be for inmates to assault them and take their firearms. Each state has a different policy, but usually COs carry pepper spray, stun guns, guns that fire high-velocity rubber bullets that are not fatal, or "billy clubs." But on each cell block, there is a "cage officer" who is a CO responsible for opening and closing cell doors and other entrances to the block. There are firearms stored inside the cage, which is heavily armored and extremely secure to make sure the guns are not taken by inmates.

## *The parole board*

The parole board is a state-sponsored panel of non-prison personnel that decides when an inmate is ready for early release. For now, keep in mind the definition of parole: the status of an offender who has been conditionally released into the community before his or her entire sentence is completed. In other words, parole is not a "free pass" out of prison. If you make parole, you are still under the jurisdiction of the DOC. You are merely being allowed to serve the remainder of your sentence in the community after the parole board decides you have met certain conditions to receive this privilege. Once you are out on parole, you must meet often with your parole officer to make sure you are obeying these conditions. If you fail to do so, a court can revoke your parole and return you to prison.

While you are preparing to go to prison, it is very important that you begin planning for parole before you even pass through the gates. Think about everything you need to do that will increase your chances for parole and to stay out of prison in the future.

# WHO'S WHO AMONG PRISON INMATES

Every prison has a "pecking order," or hierarchy, meaning that inmates who have committed certain crimes are more accepted and respected than other inmates. This is important information for you to know before you go to prison so you will know what to expect when you arrive, based on your offense. You can also use this information to see why some inmates are treated differently by other inmates; this will help you fit in and stay safe.

### The male inmate hierarchy
1.    Shot-callers who are gang leaders and have committed violent offenses against rival gangs. In a woman's prison, they too have shot-callers associated with the gangs of their "men."

2. Murderers who killed someone whom other inmates determined to have deserved to die: sex offenders, non-Americans, or homosexuals, for example.

3. Drug offenders.

4. "Outlaw" bikers convicted of numerous crimes.

5. Inmates who have committed other types of violent crimes of a non-sexual nature, such as armed robbery.

6. Thieves and burglars, including those who have committed home invasion crimes.

7. Inmates who have committed other property crimes, such as arson.

---

"This old Chester (child molester) man was creepy. He could have been anybody's grandpa. That's how he got kids to rape. Everybody just waited to get their hands on the (expletive) and give him what he had coming. But he died of some kind of sickness first. We all laughed and cheered 'cause that (expletive) wasn't going to hurt any more kids. They could have been my kids, man."

— E. P., Inmate, Wyoming

---

At the very bottom of the prison pecking order are sex offenders, child molesters in particular. Rapists are almost as unpopular. Every woman is some inmate's wife, sister, mother, daughter, or girlfriend; and forcible rape is considered cowardly and unmanly.

The prevailing prison belief is that if a man has to rape a woman to have sex, he must not be much of a man since he cannot get a woman on his own.

Child molesters, particularly those who kill their young victims, face serious risk of harm in prison. Inmates hate "baby rapers," and these inmates usually must be administratively segregated from the general population. They are in constant fear for their safety and that they will be brutally gang-raped by other inmates. This, other inmates believe, is the type of punishment that they deserve but the criminal justice system is too weak to carry out. Since these inmates are almost always serving long sentences, prison life for them is a constant state of fear. They are hated by other inmates — and probably some staff members — and have no friends. They receive visitors very rarely, if ever, except for their attorneys.

## How to tell them apart

When you get to prison, the other inmates will tell you who the sexual offenders are as well as the openly homosexual inmates who can be "bought" for favors like drugs, commissary items, and extra food in the chow hall. In a woman's prison, you will also be told who is and is not involved in lesbian relationships. You should not join in any violent actions against these inmates. This is a serious disciplinary offense and will be noted by the parole board. You would also be wise not to be friendly with them. This could put you at risk for harm because other inmates will think that you might be a "faggot" or a "sandbox rapist" (another term for child molester). This is definitely not a label you want if you want to serve your time quietly and make parole. Say what you feel you need to say about them to fit in, but never encourage or condone violence against them.

We can return to Tom's case to see where he might fit into the prison inmate hierarchy.

Tom did not intentionally commit a violent offense, although he seriously harmed his victim, the teenage girl. When he arrived in general population/medium security, Tom found that most of the inmates often bragged about being drunk or high on drugs many times. They also talked about driving cars or motorcycles while they were intoxicated, sometimes being arrested for doing so. Tom's third-offense DUI was no problem with the other inmates, but some inmates did not look kindly upon the fact that he harmed a young girl in the process. One inmate told him, "If that was my daughter I would kick your butt, dude."

Tom found that he was somewhere in the middle of the prison pecking order. He was not nearly as shunned as sex offenders but also received only minimum respect and friendship by other inmates. When Tom discussed this issue in his alcohol rehabilitation program, his counselor told him that sometimes inmates like him try to increase their status by joining prison gangs and committing crimes in prison. The counselor strongly advised him not to do this if he hoped to make parole. When Tom said that he feared prison life with little status in the hierarchy would be miserable, his counselor replied, "Then you want to get out as quickly as you can, right?"

# CHAPTER 3

## Things to Do Before You Go

Chances are that you will be in police custody in the city or county jail before you are transferred to prison. You will have only a few personal items with you in jail, much less than you will need once you get to prison. During your classification and evaluation, you will be issued items such as clothing and personal hygiene items. In this chapter, we will look at the things you need to do before you are transferred to prison. If you are unable to arrange these things while in jail, you will need someone on the "outside" to help you such as a family member, friend, pastor, or another trusted person. Here is a basic outline of the things you need to arrange before you are transferred to prison:

- Family and personal finances

- Paying your child support while you are in prison

- Arranging to pay restitution to your victim(s) when ordered by the court

- Finding a lawyer to represent you while you are incarcerated

- A practical guide to legal fees and court costs

- How to discuss appeals and new trials with your lawyer

- Obtaining your medical records before you go

- Arranging for emotional support for your family within their community

- What you can and cannot bring with you to prison

- Arranging who will receive custody of an infant you bear in prison

If this list seems overwhelming, there is no need to worry. We will look at each item individually, and you will find a helpful checklist of things to do before you are transferred to prison in the Appendix section of this book.

## YOUR FAMILY AND PERSONAL FINANCES

Even though you are in prison, life will go on for your family. This means there will be bills that need to be paid on a regular basis. Some of these are:

### *Rent or mortgage payment*

Your spouse and/or children still need a roof over their heads while you are incarcerated. It is likely that if your spouse is not working outside the home he or she will need to find a job to pay this bill. Since inmates who show good behavior and compliance with all prison rules can apply to have jobs in prison, it is important that you send as much money as possible to your family. Showing this kind of responsible behavior will not only help your family while you are in prison, but it also puts you in a favorable light with the parole board.

## Family essentials

There are other essentials your family will have to pay for every month: food, electric bills, car payments, loan payments, gasoline, clothing, school supplies for your kids, medical and dental bills, and insurance payments. Since you will most likely not be earning a steady income while in prison, the responsibility of making sure these things are paid for falls to your spouse, any of your children who are of working age, any other willing family members, your church, and possibly charities that may be able to provide assistance to your family.

It is extremely helpful if you had a savings account before you were convicted of a crime; this would allow you to use your savings to help pay these bills. If you do not have a savings account or your spouse cannot find a decent-paying job, there are churches and special charities that can help your family pay these bills, as well as government-sponsored programs like Aid for Families with Dependent Children (AFDC). To find the AFDC Web site in your state, use your law library computer's search engine and simply type "(Your state) Aid for Families with Dependent Children." Keep in mind that financially supporting your family is a major reason you should try to make parole the first time you are eligible. If you are tempted to behave in a way that will result in you receiving disciplinary action, you are less likely to make parole, and your family will remain financially strapped. Think before you act.

"When I came to prison, I had to learn that I can't get what I want when I want it. I had to plan my expenses and work hard at my job to send money home. I learned to live on five dollars a month for commissary stuff."

— *W. B., Inmate, North Dakota*

## PROVIDING FOR YOUR FAMILY WHILE IN PRISON

In case you are worried about how you can help contribute to your family's upkeep and other expenses while you are in prison, remember that you can earn money even when you are incarcerated. Prisons have jobs available both inside and outside the prison. Most prisons do not allow inmates to conduct a business via the Internet because this can be too easily abused and takes too much time. Check your inmate's manual or ask a CO to help answer questions about this in your facility. To qualify for a job, an inmate must have a record of good behavior and must meet with a panel of staff members to explain why he or she needs a job and should be allowed to work. In fact, working while incarcerated is encouraged in order to help an inmate provide money for family, a lawyer, or paying restitution to a victim as ordered by the court. Having a job will also help you fill your time during your sentence and prevent you from becoming bored with the prison's routine. If you have no one to support but yourself, you can earn money to spend at the prison commissary for hygiene products, snack foods, letter-writing materials, hobby items, and many other items that are not issued by the prison.

Do not expect to earn the same kind of money that you would earn on the outside. Prison jobs earn low pay; each state is different, but the average pay for a prison job is between $40 and $130 per month. This may not seem like much, but it could mean the difference between your child having some new school clothes or not. For your own benefit, parole boards look kindly upon inmates who work to help support their families and pay their victim's restitution.

## Child support

If you have children who are minors (younger than 18) and your spouse or another family member has custody of them, you probably have already been ordered to pay a certain amount of money each month for child support. On the outside, money you earned at your job was likely enough to pay this debt. In prison, earning prison wages, it will be much harder to earn the amount of child support that the court ordered before you were convicted and incarcerated. For example, suppose you have one child and were ordered to pay $200 per month for child support. On the outside, this is usually no problem. But in prison, you will not be able to pay this amount of money each month. Judges understand this, but you are still expected to qualify for work in the prison and send as much money as you can for child support, including any child that you or your spouse may have while you are in prison.

Making the best effort to support your children will make a good impression on the parole board. But if you spend all your work money on yourself at the prison commissary instead of sending money for child support, do not expect any slack from the parole board when they ask you why you made the taxpayers support your children instead of contributing to their support.

# LEGAL ESSENTIALS

## *Arranging to pay restitution to your victim(s)*

Along with your prison sentence, the trial judge may order you to pay restitution to your victim; this is money that goes directly to the victim of your crime to compensate him or her for any financial harm you caused. Sometimes a certain amount of the money you earn while in prison is automatically deducted from the total amount of your pay. As an example of how this works, we can take a further look at Tom's case.

As a result of Tom's crime of drinking and driving, his teenage victim was permanently paralyzed from the waist down. Her parents' insurance covered most of her medical care, but not all of it. She had difficulty getting around in a plain wheelchair because, being a small size, she had little upper body and arm strength. Her physician told her parents that it would be best if she had a motorized wheelchair, but their insurance would not cover this expense.

Thus, when Tom was sentenced, the court ordered him to pay $1,000 restitution to the child that would allow her to purchase a motorized chair. In addition, the court ordered Tom to pay the insurance deductible of $500 so the girl's parents could replace their car that was destroyed in the wreck Tom caused. When Tom arrived at the prison, he asked questions and learned all he could about the prison work programs such as how long it would be until he could apply for a job. Tom vowed to make sure his behavior and attitude qualified him for work. He was serious about making restitution to his victim as ordered by the court — not only so he might earn early parole, but also because it was the morally right thing to do.

## Finding a lawyer to represent you while you are incarcerated

Your need for legal representation does not end at the prison gates. As previously mentioned, if you were appointed a public defender for your trial, this attorney will also represent you at no charge for one appeal of your case. If this appeal is denied, you are on your own. Lawyers are expensive. Their hourly fees can be as high as $300 to $500. However, there are many lawyers who are willing to work *pro bono* (for free) if your case was grossly mishandled by the judge and/or attorneys at your trial, or if there is a serious matter of constitutional law at stake.

In addition to post-conviction appeals or motions for a new trial, sometimes inmates need an attorney to represent them regarding crimes they are accused of committing while they are in prison. For example, suppose an inmate is a member of the Aryan Brotherhood prison gang and is accused of assaulting an African American inmate in the chow hall. The accused inmate can be formally charged and tried for this new crime. If convicted, the inmate will be sentenced to additional prison time. Since this is a new charge, the judge may, in some states, appoint a public defender to represent the inmate. In other states, the inmate must take the initiative to find his own lawyer.

### Nuisance lawsuits

Another example involves inmates who wish to file lawsuits against the state's DOC for cruel and unusual treatment under the Eighth Amendment of the Constitution. Substandard medical care, the use of physical violence by corrections officers, and unwarranted long-term segregation in "the hole" are some examples of grounds for this type of lawsuit. Be cautious: When you get to prison, you will see many inmates who file frivolous lawsuits (also called nuisance lawsuits) on a regular basis that have no merit. You will have access to a law library, and you will meet many "jailhouse lawyers." These are inmates who have studied just enough law to be dangerous and annoying to other inmates who have legitimate legal issues. In many states, judges have the power to immediately dismiss (refuse to hear) these frivolous lawsuits filed by either inmates or attorneys who represent them. If you do this, it will be a part of your record in prison, and the parole board will look unfavorably upon your desire for parole. If you are a nuisance in prison, they may decide that you will also be a nuisance in society at large. The state's bar association often disciplines attorneys who continually file frivolous lawsuits for inmates.

### Where to go for help

If you need an attorney while you are incarcerated, the best place to start asking questions is with your state or county bar association. You can find phone numbers and addresses for any state's bar association in a phone book or online if you are allowed to use a computer in the prison's law library. The American Bar Association (**www.abanet.org**) provides information about the law as well as other resources such as a lawyer locator. Another place to start is by calling the National Legal Aid & Defender Association (**www.nlada.org**). These attorneys can represent you at no charge. You can discuss your case and fee arrangements, if any, either on the phone or by putting them on your visitor list and meeting with them in person. Remember, you cannot be denied the right to have an attorney to represent you, and all Miranda rights pertain to inmates as well as civilians.

## *A practical guide to legal fees and court costs*

As previously discussed, a lawyer's time is expensive. When you first meet or talk with a lawyer about representing you while you are in prison, be sure to ask questions about his or her fees. Of course, your potential lawyer knows that as an inmate, your financial resources are very limited, and first consultations with a private attorney are usually free of charge. Unless you find an attorney to represent you without charge, you will need to be honest with the lawyer about your finances. Usually an attorney will discuss with you whether you have family members who can provide monetary help, a savings account, or property that could be sold in order to pay his or her fee. The attorney will also want to know if you have a job in prison, and if the money you earn can be automatically sent to the lawyer who agrees to represent you. Honest, hard-working attorneys have reasonable fees and payment plans. If you are unsure, ask. Financial surprises are not humorous.

### *Filing a lawsuit*

Filing lawsuits can be expensive. You will probably have to pay a fee, or court cost, to file a suit unless you can prove that you have no financial resources and should be declared indigent (without an ability to pay). Under constitutional law, every person has a right to be heard in court, regardless of his or her financial standing. If you have a legitimate case that the court needs to hear, court costs can be waived. To find out more information about court costs, call or contact online your county court clerk's office. You will find this telephone number in the "government" section of the phone book, or you can use the computer's search engine by typing "(city) court clerk." Court clerks are most often found in your city's courthouse, which has a street address if you wish to mail them. This is an elected official who is a general administrator of the justice system in any given area. He or she, or a deputy court clerk in the criminal judges' office, can answer all your questions about the costs of filing a lawsuit and what sort of legal documentation you will need to provide if you are indigent. The National Center for State Courts Web site (**www.ncsc.org**) provides a list of courts in your state with contact information for the clerk. When you arrive at the home page, click "Information & Resources" and then click "Browse by state." Choose the "Court Web sites" option.

## *How to discuss appeals and motions for a new trial with your lawyer*

While you are still in the city or county jail awaiting transfer to prison, you should already be thinking about how to work with your lawyer if you plan to appeal your case or make a motion for a new trial. There are two questions for you and your attorney to consider: (1) Can you appeal your case to a higher court based upon errors of law made by the trial court judge that, if they were not made, may have resulted in a "not guilty" verdict or a different sentence? (2) Has new evidence, such as a previously unknown witness or DNA evidence, come to light that, if the jury had heard it, may have resulted in a "not guilty" verdict or a different sentence?

It is in your best interest not to talk about irrelevant points when you meet with your attorney, especially if you are paying him or her by the hour. Your counsel will not want to hear about how unfair the parole system is, why you cannot keep decongestant pills in your cell, or what the warden should do about prison gangs. Your attorney wants to know only one thing: why you believe you did not receive due process of law. This issue is the only question that a higher court will consider upon your appeal or motion for a new trial. Make it easier for everyone involved and stick to this issue alone.

---

"One of our biggest problems in processing new inmates is that they don't bring medical records with them. This means that our physicians may have to rely on the inmate's recollections of his previous health treatment, which may not be entirely accurate."

— *Warden M.*

---

## *Obtaining your medical records*

When new inmates arrive at prison, one of the most important and frustrating issues is obtaining a complete health history from them. Look at it this way: While you are in prison, life goes on as far as your body is concerned. You will still get the flu now and then, pass a painful kidney stone, or have a job-related injury. Like everyone else, you are still subject to illness and injury while you are in prison. For these conditions, you can be treated successfully either in the prison infirmary or, if your condition is more serious, in the local community hospital. You may also have a pre-existing condition that needs ongoing medical care, or you may develop a chronic illness that requires treatment in prison.

### Check Your Understanding No. 6

1. True or False:    Every inmate has a right to have a prison job to help support his family.

2. True or False:    Once you enter prison, you no longer need an attorney to represent you.

3. True or False:    You cannot be legally charged with a crime you commit in prison.

4. True or False:    Being "indigent" means that you lack the ability to pay court costs and attorney's fees.

5. True or False:    Your appeal or motion for a new trial should be based upon the jury's misconduct in your case.

We can use Tom's case as an example of these medical issues.

When Tom was a teenager, he was diagnosed with asthma. He needed to take medication and use an inhaler for this chronic illness. When Tom arrived at the state prison, he had his complete medical records from "civilian" physicians who treated his asthma and other medical concerns. The prison physicians were able to read Tom's medical history and provide him with the asthma medication that he needed.

Tom's "cellie" (cell mate) was a man named Randy who was diagnosed with diabetes two years earlier while he was already in prison. Randy told Tom that he went to the infirmary every day to have his blood sugar tested and to receive a shot of insulin. Randy also mentioned that he is having some common complications associated with diabetes, such as trouble with his eyesight and numbness in his feet. Randy told Tom that the prison physician treats him for these conditions as well as his diabetes.

One day, while Randy and Tom were eating dinner in the chow hall, another inmate told them that Lavon, an inmate who worked on the prison grounds mowing the lawn, had been injured that day. While Lavon was mowing, he turned to wave at a staff member driving to the main gate and accidentally cut off two of his toes with the mower. Tom and Randy learned that Lavon was taken to the local community hospital where he received emergency treatment for this injury. Lavon stayed in the hospital for two days and was then returned to the prison. His prison physician then gave him antibiotics to prevent infection, administered pain medication to him, and changed his bandages once each day.

"When an inmate has to go downtown to a hospital for treatment, he is subject to all necessary security precautions. He may be handcuffed and/or in leg shackles. While he's transported, two COs ride with him in the ambulance. Lots of times we have front and back chase cars, depending on the level of security needed. One, sometimes two, armed COs stay with the inmate in the hospital to prevent escapes."

*— Corrections Officer, Montana*

This may sound harsh, but remember that COs have the responsibility of maintaining security procedures even with injured inmates who leave the prison. If you must go to a civilian hospital for care, you will only be secured as your medical condition allows. In Tom's example, Lavon would not have been placed in leg shackles since his foot and toes were seriously injured. Instead, he would be only handcuffed and guarded by COs in the ambulance. Neither the COs nor the civilian medical providers will intentionally harm you.

## *Obtain all your medical records before you are transferred to prison*

This can be done by calling your physician — or having a trusted person call for you — and asking that his or her office send you a release of information form to the medical director of the prison. This is necessary for patient-doctor confidentiality; your doctor cannot release your records or talk to anyone about your medical care and needs without your written consent, even if you are an inmate of the state's DOC. Be sure to obtain all your medical records including X-rays, MRIs, and any other tests and laboratory results. Another way to provide the prison with your medical history is to sign releases of information to all doctors who have treated you while you were processed into the prison.

- **Pre-existing conditions:** For pre-existing conditions, which may require ongoing treatment while you are in prison, documentation of that condition is essential for your prison physician. In Tom's case, he had a pre-existing condition — asthma — that required daily medications. Tom did the right thing by obtaining his medical records before he went to prison. Now the prison physicians can treat him appropriately for his asthma. Pre-existing conditions include any chronic illnesses such as diabetes, cancer, asthma, chronic pain, allergies, mental illness, and substance abuse.

- **Pregnancy:** Women who are pregnant when they enter prison will have routine OB/GYN exams by the prison medical staff. If your pregnancy is somehow complicated, you will be seen by an OB/GYN physician within the local community. Also, your child will be born in a community hospital that has all necessary medical teams in place in case a delivery complication arises.

- **Illness or injury in prison:** You will receive completely adequate care at the prison infirmary or at a local community hospital. Every prison infirmary has its own pharmacy so you can receive the medications you may need. Your prison doctor will decide if your illness or injury requires more care than what is provided by the prison; only the doctor can make the decision to send you to a local hospital.

# WHAT TO BRING WITH YOU TO PRISON, AND WHAT YOU CANNOT BRING WITH YOU

Keep in mind that this is only a general list of what you can bring to prison with you. Each state has its own standards of what an inmate can legally possess. While you are being processed into the prison, the classification staff will go over your personal belongings with you to see if you can keep them or not. In most prisons, the items you can have depend upon your security and custody levels. For example, inmates classified into maximum security can have hardly anything in their cells, while minimum security inmates can have more items. One rule to remember: If you abuse it, you will lose it. The prison will issue you anything you do not have but need. This could include bars of soap, tubes of toothpaste and a tooth brush, shaving items, a small plastic comb, a writing pad, a pencil, and envelopes.

In general, these are the items that most states allow you to bring with you or have brought to you in prison:

- A religious medal and chain with a value less than $100
- A wedding band
- Eyeglasses and a case for them
- An address book
- Up to two religious books such as the Holy Bible, the Qur'an, or the Book of Mormon

- A limited number of hardcopy and paperback books
- All your legal documentation and a copy of your lawyer's case file about you
- One or two baseball-type hats
- A limited number of photographs of your family and close friends (pornographic materials of any kind are not allowed inside the prison)
- A plain deck of cards
- A hearing aid
- One watch
- Two pairs of sneakers and one pair of "regular" shoes
- One pair of work boots
- Up to five pairs of socks
- One headband or bandana, unless these items represent gang affiliation
- Up to three pairs of sweat pants with a long-sleeved top without logos
- Two athletic supporters
- Two pairs of gym shorts
- Four to six pairs of underwear
- Three pairs of pants
- Three shirts (usually T-shirts) without logos of gang affiliation, drugs, or of a sexual nature
- One pair of white sheets, one pillow and white pillowcase, and one or two blankets (these items are usually given to you by the prison)

Women inmates receive or bring with them similar items, including shampoo and sometimes makeup.

*Contraband* is anything the prison staff does not issue or that you are not allowed to bring with you to prison. All contraband items will immediately be taken by corrections officers and will either be destroyed or boxed and sent to a family member. Since what is and is not considered contraband differs by state, this will be fully explained to you when you are processing into the prison. You will also be informed about what your visitors can or cannot bring you.

The following items are generally considered contraband:

- Radios and headphones or boom boxes. Some prisons allow you to have a small radio in your cell.

- Any type of television. Some prisons allow minimum or moderate security-level inmates to earn the privilege of having a small TV in their cells based on good behavior.

- Any object or item that could be used as a weapon. This includes jackknives; metal containers; razor blades; belts; religious statues; metal or wooden medical braces; medicine of any kind; CDs; CD players or MP3 players (you may earn the privilege of having these items via good behavior); and drug-related paraphernalia such as pipes, rolling papers, or syringes.

- Candles and/or lighters.

- Empty containers.

- Anything made of glass.

# EMOTIONAL SUPPORT FOR YOUR FAMILY

Much social research on prison inmates who are released in parole has been conducted in the last decade, especially by state and federal panels. According to criminology experts, the single most important issue in cutting down the number of returning inmates is a caring, stable family to go home to. Before you board the DOC bus for your transport to prison, you should have a plan of immediate action that provides your parents, partner or spouse, and/or children the emotional support they will need while you are incarcerated.

We have already discussed how you can financially help support your family while you are in prison. Just as important is the emotional support that your family may need as they await your release. After your conviction and sentencing, and while awaiting transfer from the county/city jail to prison, this is an essential issue for you to consider and discuss with your family members. You should then begin to put your plan into action as soon as possible.

## COMMON INMATE PROCESSING FORMS

When you arrive at prison and are receiving or approving your personal items, you will be required to sign several forms: (1) your consent to have your phone calls monitored; (2) your agreement not to make any business-related calls; (3) your consent to have your incoming and outgoing mail opened and read; and (4) your agreement to have money sent to you deposited into your general prison account to be released to you as needed. Some prisons have other forms that you need to sign, such as a statement of prison rules and your agreement to abide by them.

## Check Your Understanding No. 7

1. True or False: You will not need to take your medical records because the prison physician will rely upon your own health knowledge.

2. True or False: Always tell your prison doctor about any pre-existing health conditions.

3. True or False: Even if you do not smoke, you can bring a lighter into the prison.

4. True or False: Arranging for emotional support for your family is an important part of your rehabilitation.

5. True or False: Studies have shown that when an inmate is paroled, the most important issue is going home to a caring, stable home life.

# CHAPTER 4 | Prison Rules to Know Before You Go

If this is the first time you are going to prison, it is normal to be frightened about the prison environment, the people you are going to be living with, and the rules of the prison. The formal rules will be explained to you as you in-process. These will be rules about sending and receiving mail, places that are off-limits to inmates, how to use the laundry facilities, how to use the commissary, incoming and outgoing phone calls, the expectations of the conduct of your visitors, and many other rules that may differ in other states' prisons.

Most prisons have an inmate handbook that is given to you during your classification period and explains the rules of the prison. You should read this closely, and if you are uncertain about any rule, ask a member of the classification team to answer your questions.

## THE CONVICT CODE

There is another set of rules for prison conduct, however. You will not find it in any written document, but it lurks in the shadows of prison life. Staff members are aware of the "Convict Code" of their prison and allow it to exist unless an inmate steps over the line in his behavior. In his book, Carceral defines common features of the convict code:

- Maintain loyalty to convicts over staff.

- Be a "straight-up" person by paying your debts to other convicts, being honest, and maintaining your honor as a grown man or woman.

- Do your own time. Maintain your reputation without whining.

- Never snitch about the activities of the other inmates.

- Be willing to use force to protect your interests and reputation.

- Have a lack of trust for all COs.

- Volunteer as little as possible about yourself and your personal life — no one cares.

- Do no favors and ask for none.

Carceral also points out that any book written by inmates about prison life and staff members is likely to portray these employees, especially COs, in a negative light. Books by current or former prison staff members are just as likely to portray all inmates in a negative light. The truth is probably somewhere in the middle of these two extremes. As a new inmate, you will be taught about the convict code in your prison. Sometimes you will learn it the hard way by unknowingly violating this unwritten code and being punished — usually through violence — by the other inmates.

That is why it is presented in this book, so that you will know the basics of the any prison's code before you get there.

If you are a first offender with a decent shot at early parole, the you do not want to have disciplinary reports for rules violations in your records. This is one of the first things a parole board looks for when considering parole. Remember our discussion about not associating with troublemakers and how to not become one yourself? It is sometimes hard to adhere to the convict code without violating formal prison rules. We can use Tom's case to help you understand what to do in these situations.

Shortly after Tom was settled into his housing, his cellie, Randy, said that sometime in the next few days, the African American and Hispanic inmate gang members were planning to beat him up as an "initiation" into prison life. Randy, who was white like Tom, did not want to see this happen, but he told Tom that he could not be a snitch or these gangs, especially those who had long sentences or no chance at parole, would probably kill him. Randy said that he had already broken the code by warning Tom of the coming attack and he dared not say more. Tom understood Randy's position. He knew he could not fight his way out of this threat since the other inmates were stronger, bigger, and had no qualms about a single man having to fight with five or more inmates. Quite naturally, Tom was afraid. He had met a CO who seemed like an honest, firm man who took his job seriously. Tom believed he could trust CO Fox.

He asked to speak to him privately off the unit so no one would see them talking. Tom told CO Fox about the plan to beat him up. CO Fox told him this was not unusual in their prison and the convicts as well as the victim do this "initiation" in secret in an unknown place. Tom did not tell CO Fox where he heard about the plan to harm him. He did not want to name Randy as a snitch, nor did he want to be punished by the other inmates for trusting CO Fox with what he had heard about the plan to harm him.

CO Fox told Tom that he would discuss the matter with the security chief and develop a plan to keep Tom safe during his first few weeks in prison. He advised Tom to behave as though he did not know this information, and told him that he should say things to African American and Hispanic inmates about not trusting the COs and that all the inmates were now like his family. He said that he would step up and help any inmate if needed and that he was not afraid to fight. Tom told a Hispanic inmate that his younger sister was married to a Hispanic man and lived with him in Mexico. Tom never did find out the details of the plan that CO Fox and the security chief made to keep him safe, but this whole strategy worked. Tom was not beat up, nor was he ever seriously harassed by non-white inmates. He managed to appear as if he was following the convict code and did not violate any formal prison rules.

Carceral wrote a blistering viewpoint of prison rules in his book. He likens a CO's control over inmates to a master-slave relationship. You will find that the state DOC hires a small army of COs to maintain order in the prison. The rules you must live by are necessary to correct and prevent unwanted behavior that is dangerous to the staff members and other inmates. These rules are so numerous, Carceral said, that it is impossible to obey all the rules all the time.

In an opposing position, think about what it would be like to be the warden of a prison. Your job is to make and enforce prison rules in a non-arbitrary and fair manner. Prison is not a holiday camp; they are so overcrowded in America that the number of inmates far outweighs the number of COs. Many more are needed, but DOC funding is not available. Many inmates are dangerously violent and are serving long sentences. With nothing to lose, knowing that they are not parole-eligible, the offenders pose a significant threat to staff and other inmates. Others are first offenders with shorter sentences, and the staff goals are to rehabilitate these offenders and return them safely to society.

Without fair and strictly enforced rules, a prison would quickly become anarchy and develop into a very dangerous place to live and work. Prison rules offer inmates a unique opportunity for rehabilitation: If you had not broken the rules of society, you would not be in prison. As an inmate, you can take this opportunity to prove that you can follow rules, thus providing the parole board with a very positive reason to return you to your home and family. Inmates who have many disciplinary write-ups are unlikely to be paroled.

In his book *Going to Prison?* inmate Jimmy Tayoun introduces his readers, who are almost always first offenders, to the general, formal prison rules. Take notice, however, that Tayoun was in a federal prison, not a state prison. His book is still helpful for new inmates in a state prison, but keep in mind that different prisons have their own ways of doing things, and what applies to a Maine prison may not exist in a Texas prison.

# GENERAL PRISON RULES

## *Your cell*

Inmate K.C. Carceral wrote that many of the problems in prison life are related to overcrowding. Your state builds prisons with specifications of how many inmates it can house; this is called "design capacity." For example, your institution may have been built to hold 1,500 inmates in the general population area with two inmates in a cell. Throughout America, the prison population has increased so greatly in the past 25 years that your prison may need to add two additional beds to your cell. Building prisons costs many millions of dollars in taxpayer money, and DOCs rarely have this kind of money. Also, judges and juries are handing down longer sentences for many crimes, like the "three strikes and you're out" doctrine of imprisoning people who have committed three felonies. Thus, you will most likely be living in an overcrowded situation where personal privacy is severely limited. People who live in close confines become irritable, quick-tempered, and depressed; this is common among first offenders who are not used to this lifestyle. You may have experienced similar conditions in the city or county jail where you were housed before sentencing. Since overcrowding is not an issue that you can change, keep in mind that you must still obey all prison rules and maintain your cool.

## *Cleanliness*

Inmates are responsible for keeping themselves and their cell clean. Since two inmates usually share a cell, this could be a problem if your cellie is a nasty slob. Many a fight has broken out over this exact issue. The "clean" cellie does not want to either pick up the dirty cellie's mess or get a disciplinary report for having an unclean cell. When you are taken to your cell for the first time, note its condition; is it clean or dirty? It is usually possible for you to explain your situation and your desire for early parole to your messy cellie and get him to clean up, but if your cellie has been incarcerated for quite a while and has already been denied parole, he may be disinclined to grant your request. He might follow up his words with a face slap or some other form of retaliation because you are "sucking up to the Man" (prison authorities). Think about what you might do about this situation before you go to prison and you will not be taken by surprise if it happens.

## Laundry

Every prison has rules about laundry. Usually you can exchange your bed linens each morning, and your blanket twice a week. Every prison has a laundry where inmates work to earn money by washing and drying bed linens, towels, washcloths, blankets, and kitchen linens. Depending on the rules of your prison, you may be required to wash your own clothing. Washers, dryers, and laundry soap are available in each housing unit or "block." Inmates in maximum-security housing may be allowed a few hours a week to wash their clothes while in leg shackles and with one or two COs looking on. Otherwise, these inmates could be required to send their clothing to the prison laundry.

## The commissary

Using the prison commissary is a privilege, not a right. The warden, or his or her representative, can deny or limit your access to the commissary at any time. This usually occurs when it is discovered that an inmate who obtains commissary items with his own money then re-sells them for a higher price to inmates who do not have commissary privileges, or sells them in return for "favors" from another inmate. Your commissary money consists of an account opened in your name. It includes any money you bring to prison with you, money sent to you by others, and money you earn from your prison job. Make sure you get a receipt for all money that is put into your account, and tell your visitors that the best way to provide you with money for your account is by bringing cash for you to turn over to a CO, a postal money order, or a Western Union® money order. Having family and friends send or bring you a personal check is inconvenient because the amount of the check will not be deposited in your account until it clears the person's bank; this could take as long as two weeks.

In the commissary, you can buy snacks such as candy, nuts, soup mixes, chips, and ice cream. Non-food items include letter-writing materials, shoe polish, sneakers, and gym clothes. Some prisons have an order form that you can fill out to request a certain item, such as a certain type of noodles, and if the item poses no health or security threat, you will probably be able to obtain it. Many commissaries have books and magazines that you can buy rather than borrow from the prison library if you wish to keep them. Some hygiene items are also stocked in the commissary.

## Count times

Count times are among the most strictly enforced prison rules. These are times when the COs count every single inmate. It is their responsibility to use count times and security escorts to prevent escapes and/or harm to other inmates. During count times, every inmate in general population must stand quietly in front of his cell door so the COs can clearly see him. Inmates who are on work details, in maximum security/segregation, or are being seen in the infirmary must also be counted. If an inmate cannot be accounted for, the entire housing unit or cell block will go into "lockdown mode," which confines all inmates to their cells until the missing inmate is located. During any kind of lockdown, no one, including staff, is allowed to leave or enter the prison. Crash gates that protect the security monitoring "cage" come down, and some areas of the prison, such as the warden's office and the infirmary, are also locked. These security measures are taken to prevent escapes, organized gang violence, riots, and hostage-taking situations. If the count "clears," meaning that all inmates have been accounted for, then the lockdown is lifted and everyone goes about their business. You can expect to go through counts several times a day, 365 days per year. Sure, it is a disruption in your daily routine, but remember that you are in prison.

## *Disciplinary infractions*

Every prison has a system for administering punishment for disciplinary infractions (breaking prison rules). If you want a shot at early parole, you need to avoid disciplinary reports because the parole board will ask you about them. These reports are usually called "write-ups" and can be submitted by COs, the infirmary staff, the administrative staff, the warden, and any other prison employee. When you process into prison, you will receive written and/or verbal information about different types of disciplinary infractions. Some are minor and receive a minor punishment, and some are serious and receive a serious punishment. Examples of common disciplinary violations include:

- Interfering with the overall security of the prison
- Interfering with the duties of a CO or other staff members
- Assault upon another inmate or staff members
- Threats toward another inmate or staff members
- Sexual contact with other inmates (male or female)
- Abusive language toward staff members
- Being in possession of contraband of any type
- Being in a place that is off-limits
- Refusal to obey instructions from staff members
- Making "bootleg" alcohol
- Drug trafficking
- Stealing the property of other inmates or staff members
- Failure to appear for count
- Failure to appear for work detail, a medical appointment, or a counseling appointment
- Abuse of the commissary, law library, exercise equipment, or any other government-owned property
- Violating mail and/or phone call rules
- Organized gang activity
- Encouraging/planning violence by one inmate upon another
- Conspiracy to start a prison riot
- Faking illness or injury

This is not a complete list, but it includes the most-common offenses in prisons. When you receive a disciplinary write-up, most prisons have a disciplinary panel before which you can appear and tell your side of the story. Despite other opinions, these panels are not prohibited "kangaroo courts" where you, the inmate, always lose. On the contrary, you may be able to prove that you did not commit the offense, it was strictly accidental, or that it was justified in some way such as self-defense. The disciplinary panel will determine whether the write-up was deserved, and if so, will also decide on the punishment you should receive. Most punishments involve the loss of privileges (like being unable to use the exercise room for a while), temporary loss of your prison job, a written reprimand that is placed into your permanent record for the parole board to see, or time spent in segregation — also known as "the hole" — to give you time to cool off and give some thought as to why your behavior was wrong.

When inmates use the term "the hole," they are referring to being placed into a cell by yourself, with no privileges and no contact with anyone except prison staff members. The only reading material you are allowed to have is your inmate manual and a religious book such as the Holy Bible or the Qur'an. How long you stay in the hole depends on the prison rules you broke and your conduct while you are there.

Before you go to prison, it is important that you accept the fact that you are going to lose many of the freedoms you had before you committed your crime and were convicted. Also, accept that while in prison you must follow the rules if you want your time to be as easy and brief as possible. You will meet many "problem" inmates who have a lengthy history of disciplinary write-ups.

They will most likely serve out their complete sentences or spend their lives in prison. If this does not sound like a pleasant outcome to you, prepare yourself to stay away from these inmates unless you want a fate similar to theirs.

## Mandatory education

Getting an education in prison may or may not be a rule depending on whether you are in a state or federal prison. Federal prisons now require every inmate to get a high school diploma or GED. If you are in the United States legally and English is not your native language, you will also be required to take courses in speaking, reading, and writing English. Many state prisons have these same requirements, but not all states can afford this type of education. Vocational courses such as auto mechanics, welding, carpentry, cooking, and architectural drafting may also be available to you at little or no cost. Also, many prisons allow you to obtain college degrees by correspondence or online. The general rule is that unless you spend much of your time upgrading your education, the parole board will see you as invisible.

Among inmates in general, 66 percent did not have a high school diploma, 31 percent had limited English skills, and 44 percent of those who violated their parole conditions and were returned to prison to finish serving their sentences failed to complete mandatory education requirements. In some prisons, you may not be required to complete some kind of education while serving your time, but remember that the parole board does not have to let you out, either. It comes down to this: If you want to make parole and stay out of prison, improve your educational skills at no charge while you have the chance.

**EDUCATION WHILE IN PRISON**

Federal prison inmate Michael Santos was incarcerated in 1987 for drug trafficking when he was 23 years old. In prison, Santos earned both a bachelor's and master's degree of arts. He operates his own Web site, **www.michaelsantos.net**, as a resource for those trying to understand the prison system. Based upon his outstanding disciplinary record, Santos is scheduled for release in 2013.

## Chow hall rules: formal and informal

Meals at the chow hall, like everything else in the prison routine, have rules. Do not count on sleeping in while you are in prison. Breakfast is usually served starting at 6:30 a.m. with lunch starting at 11 a.m. and dinner starting after the evening count at 5 p.m. Depending on where you are incarcerated, you might go to the chow hall by cell blocks or by unit. Inmates in personal segregation or in a segregated unit — violent offenders, for example — are not allowed to eat in the chow hall, nor are inmates in the infirmary. Your food is prepared and served by inmates who earn money from this job. Sometimes they are supervised by prison employees or by a trustworthy senior inmate. All sharp instruments, such as carving knives, are carefully watched and counted after every meal.

Disciplinary chaos can easily erupt in the chow hall; this is why so many COs are present during meals. If you get a job working in the chow hall, do not even consider trying to be funny by spitting or urinating in the food; since many diseases are passed via saliva or urine, this is a very serious rule violation that has equally serious consequences. We can use Tom's case as an example of problems that can occur in the chow hall.

## IN THE CHOW HALL

One evening when Tom and his cellie, Randy, went to dinner with their cell block, they noticed that a new inmate sat down with other Caucasian inmates at their table. One by one, each inmate took a food item from the new inmate's tray, such as a slice of bread or dessert. The new inmate did not object, but simply began to eat after his other tablemates stopped taking food from his tray. Both Randy and Tom knew that if the new inmate had objected to his food being taken by "old-timers," a fight would have broken out to teach the new guy a lesson about the prison hierarchy. Tom told Randy that when he was new to prison, he did not know that gang members all sat together in a specific part of the chow hall; a mixing of the races and/or religious groups could erupt easily into a chow hall riot. Tom said he also remembered that child molesters and rapists who were in "gen pop" (general population) received poor treatment in the chow hall. Regardless of their race or religion, other inmates constantly harassed these "undesirables," tripped them or knocked their trays out of their hands, spat in their food, or took their trays away from them. The COs are constantly on the watch for these behaviors, trying to prevent them. The same is true for suspected snitches, "fags," young inmates (called "fish"), and prison gang members who are not in good standing with the gang shot-caller for some reason. Randy replied, "The chow hall is a great place for revenge."

The food you will receive in prison is nutritionally appropriate but sometimes not very appetizing, depending on who is in charge of the kitchen crew. For inmates on special diets for medical or religious reasons, allowances can be made. For example, Jewish inmates can receive a Kosher diet, Muslims are not served pork products like ham or bacon, and diabetic inmates usually have a diet created by a prison physician.

Do not take food back to your cell from the chow hall. This rule is strictly enforced due to some inmates' ability to make "prison alcohol" from certain foods, and food is also used as a bargaining tool in various schemes among inmates. If you purchase snacks from the commissary, most prisons require you to eat them right away in the common area of gen pop before returning to your cell. If in doubt about having food in your cell, be sure to ask a CO, and consult your inmate's handbook about food rules — especially food brought to you by visitors.

## The law library

Rules about using the law library will be explained to you during your orientation and classification into the prison and will also be included in your inmate's handbook. This is another issue where the "abuse it and lose it" rule applies. If you plan to appeal your conviction and/or sentencing or make a motion for a new trial, you are entitled to use the resources of the prison law library as long as your behavior warrants this privilege and you follow the rules about using the law library. You may discover some kind of "glitch" that your lawyer overlooked in your case, or you could find a case similar to yours that had a completely different outcome. The law library contains state and federal volumes of cases decided by appellate courts, state supreme courts, and the U.S. Supreme Court; copies of the legal format you must use for filing motions and appeals; advice on what to put into your documents and what to leave out; computers and printers to prepare your legal documents; paper; and a photocopier. If you are required to pay for photocopies, you can use your commissary account to do this.

## Your mail

Rules about your incoming and outgoing mail vary from prison to prison in actual operation, but essentially you need to know before you go to prison that your incoming mail will be opened and inspected before it gets to you. Be sure to let your family and friends know not to put anything into an envelope except a paper letter or card. The CO mail inspectors will confiscate anything else found in the envelope, and you will usually be notified of this. Your outgoing mail is not read, but on the upper left-hand corner of the envelope you must put your name, prison registration number, unit or cell block number, and the prison's address. Otherwise, the letter will not be mailed. You can buy envelopes, paper, and stamps at the commissary.

In his book, Jimmy Tayoun cites an example of what is called "special mail." This refers to mail from your attorneys, politicians, court personnel, and military officials. This incoming mail is opened only in your presence to demonstrate that no one else has opened it. If you are expecting this type of mail, it should have written on the envelope, "Special mail: To be opened only in the presence of the inmate." When you correspond by mail with your attorney, the contents of that mail falls under your constitutional right to attorney-client privilege, meaning that no one can examine the contents of this mail except for you and your attorney, and no one can use its contents against you in court. This is one measure of privacy you do not lose while in prison.

Rules about receiving packages in the mail are often intricate, and you have to prepare in advance to get a package. The first step is to obtain approval from the infirmary physician, the chaplain, or your unit manager, explaining what the item is and why you want it. If your request is approved, you are allowed to forward to the sender a special form, which is to be included in the package. Most prisons require you to notify the sender in writing that you are an inmate. When the package arrives, it is opened and inspected. If the authorization slip is packed with it, you get the item. Otherwise, the item is returned. If this sounds complicated, just be sure to consult your inmate manual or ask a CO if the procedure for getting a package is similar to Tayhoun's example.

Many inmates pass the time by reading books and magazines that they receive through the mail. Softcover books can be sent to you from outside, but the package must be marked "books." If you want hardcopy books, you must have them mailed to you directly from a bookstore or from the publisher. You can subscribe to as many magazines and newspapers as you want if you have the money in your prison account to pay for them. Sometimes it is easier to have a friend or family member subscribe for you and then send you the magazine or newspaper. The catch is that any book, magazine, or newspaper can be refused by the warden if he or she feels it is not appropriate for the security and good discipline of the prison or that it promotes criminal activity. For example, written material that depicts pornography, graphic violence, hate-based or gang-based material, drug-related material, or instructions on how to make weapons will be confiscated.

## *Off-limit areas*

Rules labeling certain areas of the prison off-limits to inmates are strictly enforced for the security of the prison and the safety of staff members and inmates. There are no exceptions. For example, inmates in gen pop are usually only allowed to be in their housing area; shower rooms; the chow hall; the education building or unit; the chapel; and both inside and outside recreation areas such as the gym, TV room, or basketball court. These authorized areas are monitored by COs directly or by video cameras. Do not walk on any unpaved area of the prison compound unless a staff member says you can do so because you are performing a work detail or for another authorized reason. Being found in off-limits areas will give you a major disciplinary write-up that will be very unfavorably viewed by the parole board.

We have covered a variety of information so far in this chapter, so it is time to check your understanding of this material before we continue.

### Check Your Understanding No. 8

1. True or False: When you are uncertain about a rule, consult a CO and/or your inmate handbook.

2. True or False: The "Convict Code" is an informal set of rules designed by inmates about how to live in prison.

3. True or False: "Count times" refers to the length of your sentence.

4. True or False: It is your friends' and family's responsibility to learn about prison mail rules.

5. True or False:    You receive one warning if you are off-limits before you get a write-up for doing it again.

## Recreation rules

Even rules about recreation will be an important part of your life in prison. The majority of prisons today have both inside and outside recreation areas. This can include a special area for hobbies and making crafts that inmates can legitimately sell to earn money. You will also find a weightlifting room, a music room, and a game room with billiard tables, foosball tables, chess, dominos, checkers, backgammon, and cards. Outside, there are usually basketball courts, a boxing arena, and perhaps even a baseball and/or football field. Taking advantage of the recreation opportunities in your prison is a privilege, not a right — just like the commissary. There are rules about violence, gang fights, and betting on the outcome of any kind of game. You will lose your recreational time by abusing or destroying equipment; this will also make you unpopular with inmates who depend upon this equipment for their own recreation time.

## Telephone calls

Making telephone calls in prison can be as complicated as sending and receiving mail and packages. Before you go to prison, make sure you and your attorney have an arrangement with the prison staff whereby you can have confidential, unrecorded telephone time with your children or partner. Other than this, depending on your prison's rules, you can usually make telephone calls by using coins from your account or calling collect to someone who will accept the charges. Changes in this system are, however, already underway; in the near future, you can make phone calls by pre-paying with money you earn or that is sent into a special phone call account. This method is the least expensive way of calling your family and friends.

Whichever way you pay for your phone calls, they are limited to 15 or 20 minutes, after which the line goes dead. This prevents inmates from clogging the phone lines, especially inmates who are in some way intimidating to other inmates. Arguments about phone call times can turn into major fights. You are not allowed to conduct any type of business, legitimate or illegal, over the phone. For example, Mafia leader John Gotti (who died in prison of cancer) was said to have run his illegal empire from prison phone calls. Whether this is a prison legend or was actually true, you will find strict limitations on who you can call, their relationship to you, where they live, and your reasons for calling them. For example, you will not be able to call an inmate in another facility, a person who is known by law enforcement personnel to be involved in criminal activity, or the victim of your own crime.

## *Visitors in prison*

Visitors in prison are very carefully screened and monitored. Before you are transferred to prison, make a list of people you would like to have on your visitor's log, such as family members (including your children), your attorney, close friends, a religious leader, and a legal investigator. Your visitor's list must be evaluated through a background check and approved by prison staff members before the list becomes final. Unapproved visitors will not be allowed access to you for your safety and for prison security. Your inmate's handbook will explain how many visits you are entitled to each month and the code of conduct that your visitors must obey. Some prisons, for example, allow you to hug and/or kiss a visitor — but not to excess — and to hold hands. Prison visiting rooms are usually monitored by a number of COs to prevent the passing of contraband from a visitor to an inmate. It is your responsibility to make sure your visitors obey the rules about their conduct. Accepting contraband from a visitor usually results in disciplinary consequences for you and the removal of that visitor from your approved list.

If you wish for your children to visit you, most prisons have smaller, more private areas where you can play with your children. If you choose not to have your children see you behind prison bars, your decision will be honored.

In prisons with higher security levels, inmates and visitors cannot touch each other. They are separated by a glass partition and must speak to each other through special telephones that may be monitored by COs. Visitors are subjected to "pat-down" searches to prevent drugs, weapons, or other contraband from passing into the prison. In these prisons, security always overrides family bonds.

### Conjugal visits

You may have previously heard the term "conjugal visit." Not all prisons allow these visits, and those who do allow them make them fairly brief in duration. A conjugal visit with your legal spouse takes place in a private, unmonitored room with a comfortable bed where the two of you can have sexual contact for up to an hour. The purpose of conjugal visits is to allow you to maintain your close bond of intimacy with your legal spouse — a crucial element, many researchers believe, in motivating you to behave well in prison, make parole, and stay out of prison in the future.

In some prisons, inmates are allowed to marry while they are incarcerated. But other states forbid inmates to marry because marriage is a legal contract, and prisoners lose the right to enter into contracts while in prison. If you are allowed to marry in prison or are legally married when you come to prison, you may gain the privilege of conjugal visits by demonstrating good behavior. For example, one of the "Manson Family" members, Charles "Tex" Watson, who murdered as many as nine people on the command of Charles Manson, married in prison and now has several children. All of his paroles have been denied.

## Check Your Understanding No. 9

1. True or False:    You can use your recreation time to create crafted items that you can sell in prison-run stores.

2. True or False:    Recreation yards are a good place to settle scores against rival gang members.

3. True or False:    You are not allowed to make phone calls to anyone but family members.

4. True or False:    Your visitors must be approved through a background check before they are allowed to see you.

5. True or False:    Displays of physical affection are against the rules in every U.S. federal or state prison.

# RISKY BUSINESS: STAYING SAFE IN PRISON

Now that you are familiar with some of the formal rules as well as the unwritten convict code, we need to focus on some even more obscure prison rules and procedures that you normally would not find out about until you arrive in your cell block. Even then, details of these shadowy rules and practices are rarely discussed. It is best if you read this information now so you will not become a victim of the roughest parts of prison life.

If you were sentenced to prison on a first offense and have been held in the city or county jail while awaiting your trial, conviction, and transfer to prison, the first thing you will discover is that jail is extremely different from prison. People are always coming and going from jail. They make bond and are then released until their trial ends, their charges are dropped, or they finish serving their sentence in jail and are released. In prison, you will be surrounded by pretty much the same population for several years. When this happens, alliances, factions, and groups form centered on race, religion, national origin, and life interests. We can use Tom's case to illustrate this issue.

## STAYING SAFE IN PRISON

When Tom was new to prison, he found that Randy, his cellie, was a guy he could talk to, and that Randy would help him learn the basics of behavior that was "prison proper" among inmates. The first thing Randy told Tom was to forget everything he learned about being incarcerated in jail. Randy explained that prison was a society made up of people who were violent, people who committed sex crimes, stole property, used and dealt drugs, lied, and deceived others to get what they wanted — and that they kept right on doing these things in prison.

Tom asked, "If I have to live with these people, how can I be rehabilitated? It seems like I'll come out of prison worse than when I went in." Randy replied that Tom would basically have to come up with ways to rehabilitate himself because the inmates he lived with were not going to help him. Randy said, "When I robbed that convenience store, I was high on crack. I shot at the clerk and was lucky that I did not hit him, or I would be in here for murder for the rest of my life. If I want drugs in prison, there are ways to get them. But I do not. I want to go home to my family. So I go to drug counseling as much as I can, and I got my high school diploma. I passed the exam as an apprentice welder."

Randy told Tom that among the inmates, it is hard to stay safe in prison if you are not a member of a gang. "Solo" inmates were unprotected by other inmates from rival gangs. Randy himself was not a gang member. He chose to be solo to increase his chances of making parole at his second hearing before the board. He told Tom that staying safe in prison was much harder than staying safe in jail because prisons are over-crowded and the COs cannot be everywhere at once. "Bad things can, and do, happen in prison. Get used to this fact and keep yourself as safe as you can," Randy advised Tom.

# *Pointers*

In general, there are some pointers about staying safe in prison. Study them carefully before you go because they may save your life in the end.

Although state DOCs try to keep both male and female violent offenders out of gen pop and confined to maximum-security units or "super-max" facilities, this is not always possible due to a lack of funding and prison over-crowding. You may find yourself housed in the same cell block as some violent offenders. Always remember that if they were dangerous on the outside, they are likely dangerous on the inside.

### *Avoid disruptive inmates*

If you see a crowd of inmates gathering in the chow hall, the common room, or on the recreation field, stay away. Chances are good that some kind of violence — such as an assault on other inmates, drug trafficking, retaliation for inmates who "punked" them or dealt dishonestly with them, retaliation against a suspected snitch, or other rules violations — are being planned. This kind of activity is usually gang-related. If you have been smart and stayed solo, keep yourself among other solo inmates who you can trust; all of you must mind your own business and keep out of the way of brewing trouble. When violence erupts in these crowds, the illegal homemade weapons come out and the fighters do not care who they hit, even accidentally. Stay out of their way and let the COs do their jobs.

Research suggests that inmates usually go through stages of disruptive behavior, beginning with being non-disruptive when they first enter prison, to "blooming" into problematic inmates, and finally becoming chronic, dangerous troublemakers. You can decide right now, as you read this book before you go to prison, not to be another statistic. You can decide to not be a habitually dangerous inmate. If you are a first offender with a fairly light sentence, becoming hardened by prison life is not in your best interest. This will cause you to be denied parole and serve out your entire sentence, and it puts you at high risk to commit other crimes and be returned to prison. Make your decision now and stick with it no matter what happens. Remember, you have a life waiting for you outside of prison.

### Avoid discussing your personal life

Do not talk too much about your personal life. Other inmates do not care about your marriage, your kids, your former job, things you have done wrong but were not discovered, where you live, or your sexual history. Some inmates seek this information only to use against you when they need something from you and can use what you told them to blackmail you or threaten you into doing something illegal or against prison rules for them. Trust in others is hard to come by in prison, and betrayal of trust is commonplace. Make sure you get to know someone well before you reveal any personal information about yourself. Trust no one, at least until you have settled in and have a good idea about who to definitely avoid and who you feel safe with. You do not get to choose the company you keep — your cellie is chosen *for* you, not *by* you. Cellies tend to talk with each other often if they get along well, especially after lights-out when everyone is feeling more than a little lonely. Hopefully your cellie will be someone you can trust with your personal life, but just because you live together within a small space, do not assume that your cellie is a decent person. He or she may be fundamentally good, but remember where you are. Prison is not known for housing decent people; be careful.

### Mind your manners when necessary

Treat staff members with courtesy, but do not try to become their buddies. The COs do not want you as a friend; they are there to do a job and nothing more. If you are anything more than polite to any staff member, other inmates will think you are "sucking up to the Man" to get special treatment for being a snitch. This will come back to haunt you because snitches are not safe in gen pop.

Never transfer gossip about other inmates — what they may be planning to do or have done on the outside. Focus only on doing the things that you know you need to do to make parole as quickly as possible, and let the long-termers settle their own matters.

Watch your mouth. When you are in such a closed society as a prison, arguments can break out over simple things like phone calls, work details, what channel to watch on the common room TV, and who got a bigger piece of corn bread in the chow hall. Tempers are often short among inmates, and you do not know what may be happening in another inmate's life that may make him irritable. Cursing at another inmate could lead to a full-blown fight, and it will not be a fair fight because you live among people who usually cannot control their impulses. Even if you mean only to tease another inmate with good nature, you cannot predict how he or she will respond. Prison is not the place to be the "class clown." Learn to govern your words before you go to prison, and do not try to talk tough when you are there because you most likely are not, compared to the other inmates.

### Walk away from a fight

If you possibly can, walk away from a fight. Some inmates have no qualms about fighting anyone and everyone just to gain a "rep" as a tough guy. You will find that instead of starting a fight with a gang shot-caller or his higher-up members, some inmates deliberately pick fights with new inmates who are still solo or are still anxious and afraid about being in prison for the first time. If you are challenged, a safe thing to say is, "Hey man, I don't have a problem with you and don't want one. Let's just cool it, okay?"

If you are unable to walk away from a fight, try to make sure you are in a place where COs are either present or monitoring the area by a video camera. The corrections staff knows that new, first offenders are likely to be challenged to fight, and they will be nearby to break it up. *Never* be the one to throw the first punch; let the other inmate do it and suffer the consequences of disciplinary action. You may have to take a black eye or cut lip, but in the end you will have done the smarter thing by staying out of fights. Inmates learn who they can pick on to provoke a fight and who will walk away with disinterest and dignity.

"If you're inside, you have got to learn to fight one way or the other. These new guys, they come in here and talk badass just asking someone to take them on. When it happens, the newbie ain't so tough anymore. If you have the right 'don't (expletive) with me' attitude, maybe you will not have to fight. I'm in here for murder, so I don't give a (expletive) who I hurt, or who hurts me. If I could tell new fish just one thing, it would be to shut the (expletive) up until you know the ropes."

— R. R., Inmate, Wyoming

### Keep whining to a minimum

Be cautious in complaining about an inmate to another inmate or to a CO. This is generally viewed as snitching or whining. For example, you may find that your cellie is not concerned with his or her personal hygiene and has very bad body odor that surrounds you all night, every night. If you tell this to another inmate, you can be sure it will get back to your cellie, who will not take it kindly. If you tell this to a CO, chances are good that your cellie will be told about the purposes of soap and deodorant and instructed to put these things to good use. This may solve the problem, but if word gets out on the unit grapevine that you told a CO your cellie stinks, you may find yourself with yet another problem — whining to a CO about a fellow inmate. Once you get to know your cellie and other inmates in your unit, it is best to "man up" and address the issue directly, but not in an insulting manner. This will gain you some respect as well as a cell that smells better. Some problems with other inmates you will just have to live with. Remember where you live, and with whom.

### Mentally ill inmates

A very hot social and political topic has always been the housing of mentally ill inmates in prison. Although these inmates have been convicted of crimes, they can also be very unpredictable, even dangerous. Some common characteristics of mentally ill inmates are:

- They have hallucinations or delusions (false thoughts) that others are going to harm them. They attempt to harm others before *being* harmed.

- Their thoughts may be confused and disorganized, making their behavior unpredictable.

- They have little self-insight and poor judgment about what is happening around them.

- They sometimes attempt suicide due to depression.

- They can be very anxious and afraid of their environment.

- They often refuse psychiatric medications that would help them with these symptoms.

- Their behavior may become so disruptive or dangerous that they must be sent to a psychiatric hospital.

When you arrive at prison, these inmates are usually easy to spot by their strange behavior. Since they are so impulsive and possibly dangerous, it is best to stay safe by keeping away from mentally ill inmates. This is not said in a mean-spirited way, but this is a section about staying safe in prison; sometimes mentally ill inmates, especially those who refuse medications, can be harmful to you.

Before we move on, it is time to check your understanding of the material presented in this section.

## Check Your Understanding No. 10

1. True or False: Jail conditions are pretty much the same as prison conditions.

2. True or False: If you see a crowd of inmates gathering, go and join them to see what it is all about.

3. True or False: The only person you can really trust in prison is your cellie.

4. True or False: The best way to establish your "rep" is to talk tough when you first arrive in prison.

5. True or False: Mentally ill inmates are no danger to others because they take medications.

---

"Let us not look back in anger, or forward
in fear, but around us in awareness."

*--James Thurber*

---

# 5 Necessary Information You Won't Find at Orientation

This chapter may be hard for you to read. It is not meant to scare you. It is meant to tell you the truth about the darkest sides of living in prison, rules that can help to protect you, and to inform you how you can protect yourself. Since you are reading this before you go to prison, you will not be surprised when bad things happen to others, and you can take steps to help make yourself safer in prison.

When hundreds of men or women are locked up together over a long period of time and rules govern every aspect of their lives, some bad things are bound to happen. Not everyone will get along, and some inmates will disregard some of the prison rules. For instance, some contraband items — such as drugs and weapons — are smuggled into prison no matter how hard the COs work to keep them out. Because of the stress of being behind bars and without the freedom to do what you want, when you want, tempers are short and arguments can turn deadly. Sex is a normal human physical drive, and the desire for sex does not go away just because you are locked up. In a closed, locked-down society like prison, sex can either be consensual or forced. To some prison inmates, it makes no difference.

If you were to conduct a survey of all the first offenders in America — both men and women — and ask them what they were most afraid of going to prison, it is very likely that they would specify violence and rape. These two things happen in every prison in the United States. Although the Eighth Amendment prohibits cruel and unusual punishment, and one of the primary jobs of COs is to keep inmates from being harmed by other inmates, drugs, sex, violence, and gang activity continue to occur every single day in our prisons. Our purpose here is to speak openly about things you will not hear from prison staff members. The only real prevention of harmful acts is awareness and honesty.

## PRISON GANGS OVERVIEW

For your safety, you need to know that wherever you are going to serve your prison time, gangs are everywhere. In many prisons, gang members openly flaunt their tattoos, wear their "colors," and set themselves against other prison gangs. Male and female inmates are prohibited from gang activity in prison. However, convicts, especially violent long-termers, are not known for their obedience to rules. COs, the security chief, the warden, and other staff members are well aware that there is gang activity in their prison. They can usually keep such activity to a minimum, but it is never completely eliminated. In fact, you should keep in mind that staff members know much more than they are given credit for. Instead of unwisely calling attention to what they do and do not know, they simply watch, listen, and when necessary, intervene to protect the safety of all inmates. COs are specially trained in recognizing gang activity, such as planned violence against another gang, drug and weapon trafficking, gambling, and forced sexual acts. They also know the meaning of every tattoo, every hand sign, every color, and every phrase that identifies an inmate as a gang member. Since every prison gang has a shot-caller who directs all activities of the gang, the COs, security chief, and warden also know the identity of every shot-caller in the prison.

Gangs are the underground machinery that runs the prison drug trade, weapons deals, organized fights with rival gangs, planned rapes, and (usually) prison riots. It could be argued that if our correctional system could eliminate gangs, prison would be a much safer place. This, however, is nothing but wishful thinking. Prison gangs have always existed and will continue to exist. It will be helpful for you to be able to identify the major gangs you will most likely find in your prison.

# GANG PROFILES

### The Aryan Brotherhood

The Aryan Brotherhood is a vicious and brutal white supremacist gang that originated in San Quentin prison in 1967. It was originally formed to protect white individuals from African American and Hispanic groups in the prison.

The term "Aryan" refers to Adolph Hitler's name for his "Master Race" that consisted only of white Germans, preferably blonde and blue-eyed. Although this gang operates in relative secrecy outside prison, inside prison the gang is extremely visible. The

AB considers the murder of a non-white person (in or out of prison) to be a heroic act for which they are willing to serve life in prison without parole, or even receive the death penalty. The gang particularly hates African Americans and Jews, although they also target Hispanics, Muslims, Asians, and homosexuals. They celebrate the birthday of Adolph Hitler each year on April 20.

The AB has many spin-off groups, such as the youth gang called the Skinheads, the Posse Comitatus, and the Aryan Nation. They regard white people who marry outside their race to be "race traitors" and mark them too for retaliation, even murder. Among researchers and the Department of Justice, the Aryan Brotherhood is considered to be the most dangerous gang in America today.

You will be able to easily identify AB members when you arrive in prison. The first thing you will notice is that AB members always hang together and never mix with non-white inmates in the common room, the chow hall, or recreation areas. You will hear them refer to non-whites only with vulgar racial slurs. Since most of them are in prison for crimes of violence or weapons charges, they talk about violence often — mostly, what they have done to non-whites and white race traitors. Then there is their physical appearance: They are usually short-haired, heavily muscled, and tattooed with AB symbols like swastikas and other Nazi symbols. If you see an AB gang member with a spider web tattooed over his elbow, this means that he has killed an African American or a Jewish person. This tattoo is the highest badge of honor among AB members.

In prison, the Aryan Brotherhood deals mostly in contraband weapons, violence against non-whites, and staking out prison territory where only white inmates are allowed to be. The AB occasionally deals in contraband drugs, but most AB gangs avoid the use or selling of drugs, believing that drugs are only for the "garbage races." They are, however, fond of prison-made alcohol. As with any gang, only the AB shot-caller identifies a non-white target of violence and sends a member to "do the job." The shot-caller also organizes gang fights and decides what kind of weapons will be made or smuggled in for the gang.

When you arrive in prison, and if you are white, at some point the AB will approach you about joining with them. If this happens, it means that you have been "sized up" by the gang and they are satisfied that you are purely white, of a size and build good enough to hold your own in a fight, that you are not a homosexual, that you do not associate with non-white inmates, and that you can keep your mouth shut about gang business.

Be very careful how you respond to an approach by an AB member. There may be no "right" answer to this question. If you express interest in joining them, you will instantly make deadly enemies of the non-white prison gangs. Even though AB members take oaths to protect each other, not even your gang brothers can be everywhere at once. On the other hand, if you refuse the AB's interest in you, they will most likely mark you as a race traitor or a homosexual. They will become your enemy — a very undesirable position for you. We can use Tom's case to illustrate this point.

## THE ARYAN BROTHERHOOD

A month after Tom arrived in prison, an Aryan Brotherhood member named Hunter approached Tom and told him that Silver Fox, the AB shot-caller, wanted to arrange a meeting with him. Tom had been observing all the prison gangs and had been warned about them by Randy, his cellie. Tom noticed that Hunter had the telltale spider web tattoo on his left elbow, so he knew that Hunter was not afraid of violence. He told Hunter that he would accept Silver Fox's invitation to sit with the gang in the chow hall that evening. When Tom met Silver Fox, he noticed that the shot-caller had spider webs on both elbows, and that they were darkened inside the web; Tom knew this meant that Silver Fox claimed to have killed numerous African Americans and Jewish people.

Silver Fox asked Tom how he felt about non-whites and the issue of mixing the races to produce "mongrel" babies. Tom knew he must be extremely careful how he spoke with this dangerous shot caller. He responded that he did not approve of biracial kids and that each race should stick to their own kind. He emphasized that he preferred to be around other white people. Hunter, the gang's "lieutenant," asked Tom if he could handle himself in a fight. Tom carefully explained that since he was a first offender and had a shorter sentence than many of the other inmates, he did not want to be involved in fights because he wanted to make parole. He also said that his wife was pregnant (which was not true) and that he wanted to be a real father to this child. Silver Fox asked Tom if he would back up other whites in fights or disagreements with COs. Tom said that he would, but he would not do this for non-white inmates. Tom said he did not want trouble with anyone, but that he was not afraid to defend himself and would never snitch on anyone, especially a white inmate.

Silver Fox told Tom that he felt Tom was a "white man of respect" and that the AB would not harass him. If Tom needed help from the AB, all he had to do was come to him or Hunter. After dinner, Tom felt relieved; he had made a good impression with the AB but did not feel compelled to join them in violence against non-whites. Randy, who had been through the same ordeal with the AB, advised Tom to keep his word not to snitch about AB plans for violence or obtaining weapons, to avoid friendships with non-whites, and if he saw trouble about to erupt between the AB and a rival gang, to "get himself elsewhere."

Tom's case is a good example of how to be on decent terms with a prison gang without actually joining in the gang's illegal activities; this applies to all prison gangs. Yes, you may find yourself walking a very fine line no matter what your race, religion, or sexual preference. This is a reality of living in prison.

## The Latin Kings

The Latin Kings are the most powerful and oldest Hispanic gang in America. They originally began in Chicago as a social group that acted to rise above racism and promote Puerto Rican values, heritage, and traditions but eventually became a well-organized criminal gang. They are associated with the powerful Mexican Mafia and the Vice Lords — both well-known Hispanic gangs.

Outside prison, the Latin Kings specialize in drug trafficking, drive-by shootings, and weapons dealing in schools to recruit young members. In prison, they compete with the Aryan Brotherhood for the weapons trade and for control of the prison drug trade. They too have identifying tattoos that they get at a young age. A young male's first tattoo marking him as a Latin King is a cause for celebration. Along with their tattoos, many Latin King members wear black bandanas around their heads — a symbol of death in their culture.

The Latin Kings compete with other Hispanic gangs, both in and out of prison, for territory or "turf." In prison, like other gangs, they will quickly attack non-gang members who stray into their territory in the chow hall, common room, and recreation yards. To keep others, especially the COs, from knowing too much about their illegal activities, the Latin Kings tend to primarily speak Spanish. You will be able to identify these gang members by their almost exclusive use of Spanish and their preferred colors of black and gold. If you are non-Hispanic and/or do not speak Spanish, you will be seen suspiciously as an "outsider." This is a nasty-tempered gang that verbally abuses others in Spanish and their own Spanish-based slang terms. This gang also has more female inmates than other gangs. Unless you are a Spanish-speaking Hispanic, it is wise for you to keep your distance from the Latin Kings.

### The MS-13

MS-13, also known as *La Mara Salvatrucha*, first originated in El Salvador and spread through the United States by way of Los Angeles. The MS-13 is becoming one of the most dangerous gangs in America. Curiously, this gang is usually friendly with the Aryan Brotherhood. Both gangs agree to stay out of each others' territory and illegal business, even in prison. Still, MS-13 is a vicious gang that thinks nothing of assaulting or killing rival gang members, especially African American gangs. Outside prison, this gang sells weapons and drugs in the Southwest, and in prison they continue these "businesses."

MS-13 is very active on the outside in recruiting young gang members in schools, and then using these youths as drug runners inside the schools. Thus, if you meet a young, Hispanic first offender, keep your distance. Violence, even murder, is a requirement for full membership in MS-13 both in and out of prison.

### The Crips

The Crips are an African American gang that, on the outside, are heavily involved in drug trafficking, extortion, drive-by shootings, assault, and murder. They have a presence all over the United States but are especially active in South Central Los Angeles. In many prisons, you can identify them by the wearing of their "colors," usually consisting of a blue bandana. Some prisons have forbidden the wearing of colors inside the prison to cut down on gang rivalry and violence.

### The Bloods

Another African American gang, the Bloods, is the hated enemy of the Crips. They represent their affiliation by wearing red bandanas, the opposite color of their rival gang. Both in and out of prison, they compete for control of the drug trade. Young recruits are first taught to fight before they are "jumped in" to the gang. In prison, young first offenders are required to fight either a white inmate or a Crip. The Bloods are outnumbered in and out of prison by the Crips; to make up for this, Bloods are notorious for being vicious and efficient street fighters. No rules, no mercy, and no surrender.

A word of caution: If you are a new African American inmate, male or female, chances are very good that after a period of evaluation by the shot-callers of the Crips and the Bloods, you will be approached about "hanging" with one of these gangs. More than even the Aryan Brotherhood, these gangs are extremely serious about obtaining new members in prison. If you choose to hang with one, the other will be your worst enemy. Be prepared to either make a choice about your gang affiliation or respond as Tom did in our last case scenario. "Solo" African Americans in prison are not popular and receive no protection from either the Crips or the Bloods. You will be in a difficult position, so watch your back because no one else will.

### Triads and Tongs

Although Asian gangs — usually referred to as triads or tongs — are not often openly active in prison, you should still be aware of them. They are identified by a dragon tattoo on either arm. In and out of prison, these gangs are mostly involved in drug trafficking. They often try to intimidate other inmates by flashing martial arts moves. But do not worry — most of this is fake, just to scare you. While most tong or triad inmates are not very good fighters, do not take any chances. You might find yourself fighting against a shot-caller who is the "real thing."

It is time to check your understanding about prison gangs.

## Check Your Understanding No. 11

1. True or False:    Gangs that are active outside prison are not active inside prison.

2. True or False:　Prison gangs are formed around race and ethnic backgrounds.

3. True or False:　The most dangerous gang today in prison is the Aryan Brotherhood.

4. True or False:　Since gangs are suspicious of strangers, it is unlikely that you will be approached about joining a gang.

5. True or False:　Prison gangs are mostly made up of "long-termers" who do not expect to be paroled.

Perhaps you have noticed that this section did not discuss the involvement of Italian inmates in prison gangs. This is because most criminologists do not see the Italian Mafia as a gang. Rather, they are an organized criminal society with designated leaders and specific activities that not only include drugs and weapons dealing, but also gambling, prostitution, stock market fraud, and corrupt workers' union activities. The Mafia refers to itself as *La Cosa Nostra*, which means "Our Thing." This organization does not call attention to itself as gangs do. There are no tattoos, no "colors," and no shot-caller who is well known among both inmates and prison staff. The Mafia depends upon *omerta*, their code of silence. While prison gangs brag about their illegal activities and how bad they are, the Mafia merely watches and waits in silence.

If you are an Italian American, chances are that you will not become a "made guy" — a murderer for the Mafia — by prison Mafia members. These inmates generally know each other very well, even before they were incarcerated. Just being of Italian or

Sicilian descent is not enough to vouch for your entrance into *La Cosa Nostra.*

# PRISON DRUGS OVERVIEW

Contrary to what people would like to believe, there are drugs in prison. These drugs fall into several categories:

- Drugs that are smuggled into prison by visitors, corrupt prison employees, or corrupt attorneys. These people are paid well by the prison shot-caller.

- Drugs that are manufactured in prison by inmates.

- Drugs that are illegally obtained through the prison infirmary.

As we discussed before, it is a serious violation of prison rules for a visitor to smuggle contraband of any kind for an inmate. Yet, this is how the great majority of drugs get into prison. Feeling pressured by friends, loved ones, or fellow gang members to smuggle in drugs — usually heroin, LSD ("blotter acid"), MDMA (Ecstasy), and marijuana — visitors come up with many clever ways to pass drugs to an inmate during visiting hours. This includes using condoms to insert the drugs into their rectum, vagina, or the inside of their cheeks and hidden inside a child's diaper. Visitors are civilians and not under the immediate control of the prison security staff, so the COs cannot do full body cavity searches on them as they can with inmates. However, once it becomes known that a visitor has smuggled drugs into the prison, the local police can arrest that person for drug trafficking.

The overwhelming majority of prison staff members and attorneys who visit inmates are honest people. But it is unrealistic to say that there are not some "bad apples" among these people who seek to gain money from the sale of drugs in prison. An average corrections officer makes about $30,000 a year (before taxes) and almost always has a family to support. The lure of making easy additional income through the prison drug trade has a very strong appeal that is hard for some COs to resist. When they are caught, as they almost always are, not only are their careers over, but they also find themselves standing trial for drug trafficking.

Since attorneys are generally paid well, it is difficult to understand why they would risk disbarment and criminal charges to make a few more bucks in the prison drug trade. The only reasonable answer is that these people are seeking power and control rather than money. Corrupt attorneys need and enjoy the thrill that comes with taking risks. Being involved with drug trafficking makes them feel powerful and superior to others. Put simply, they enjoy danger and the "high" that comes with outwitting others.

## Drug profiles

### Pruno

Pruno, or prison wine, is what inmates call the alcohol they make secretly in their cells. This is a practice handed down from inmate to inmate. All an inmate needs is some fruit, bread, sugar, and water, plus a container that can easily be hid out of the COs' sight. In time, this mixture ferments into alcohol. It has a horrible taste, but does have an intoxicating effect. As a first offender who hopes to make parole, making pruno is something you do not want to be involved in. It is usually discovered when COs observe inmates acting as if they are intoxicated, when someone such as a cellie snitches on the "brewer," or when the nasty substance is discovered in a cell search. Punishment for making pruno is serious, and chances for parole are negatively affected; not only should you not make pruno, but you should not buy or drink it either. Just remember that it is equally serious offense to make it as to buy or drink it.

### Decongestants

Decongestants are the most abused of the drugs that are stolen from the prison infirmary. When taken in large quantities, they produce a weird kind of "high" that is similar to uppers such as methamphetamine and crack cocaine. The down side to abusing decongestants like this is that you could eventually go into liver or kidney failure and die. Inmates with colds or allergies are often prescribed decongestants. Many prisons have changed their rules about inmates keeping these pills in their cells. Recent changes in some DOCs' procedures make inmates come to the infirmary for "pill pass" instead of being allowed to keep and sell decongestants in their cells.

In prison, there are few legal drugs in the infirmary that inmates do not abuse and/or sell to other inmates. Narcotics such as morphine, heroin, and marijuana are at the top of the "most wanted" list, but even drugs like antihistamines, antidepressants, and non-narcotic pain medications are secreted out of the infirmary and into the hands of waiting inmates who are desperate to change their moods, if only for a short period of time. During pill pass, the medical technician or nurse who gives an inmate their medication makes him open his mouth while she looks under his tongue and in his cheeks to make sure that he has really swallowed the medication.

## NARCOTICS

In everyday slang, the word "narcotics" technically refers to drugs that cause central nervous system depression, called "downers." Drugs like cocaine and methamphetamine are central nervous system stimulants, called "uppers." We tend to use the term "narcotics" to combine all illegal drugs. State and federal laws solve this problem by charging a person with "possession of controlled substances."

It is not only unwise, but also dangerous, for you to either buy or sell medications. Not only do you not know what you are really getting from another inmate, you also do not know the side effects of a large amount of any medication. We can use Tom's case as an example of this serious issue.

## UNFORSEEN DANGERS

One day, Tom and Randy were sitting in the common room watching television. Another inmate, Dante, joined them, but after about 10 minutes, Dante began to complain that his left arm was going numb. In only a few seconds, Dante collapsed on the common room floor. Tom ran to grab the nearest CO while Randy stayed with Dante. The emergency medical team arrived quickly to take Dante to the infirmary, where the physician found that Dante had suffered a severe heart attack. The physician had been treating Dante, who was 60 years old, for a heart condition prior to this time. Dante was stabilized in the infirmary and then rushed to the local hospital where he died in the emergency room 30 minutes later.

An autopsy showed that Dante died from an overdose an asthma medication that comes in an inhaler. Dante did not have asthma. The normal dose of this medicine is two "puffs" as needed, up to only four cause of Dante's death, the entire unit was put into lockdown conditions. The security chief ordered strip searches and cell searches of every inmate in the unit. A CO discovered a stash of these medicated inhalers hidden in the cell of an inmate named Esteban who was a member of the MS-13 Hispanic prison gang. Esteban had been selling inhalers to other inmates. He got them from an inmate who did have asthma. Jamal, Dante's cellie, told the security chief that Dante used stolen inhalers to get high. What Dante did not know was that among people who have even minor heart problems, an overdose of asthma medication can cause serious, even fatal, heart attacks. Tom and Randy told the security chief that when Dante joined them in the common room, he seemed a little wobbly on his feet. Esteban was charged with drug trafficking and being an accessory to manslaughter, both felony crimes for which he will do additional time in prison.

## SEX IN PRISON

Although sexual contact of any kind is forbidden by all prisons' rules, the truth is that it still happens. Both men and women inmates engage in consensual sex or violent rape. In 2003, Congress passed the Prison Rape Elimination Act, or PREA. This act required a complete evaluation of the problem of prison rape and the development of national policies to prevent sexual violence in prison. Under the terms of PREA, every prison in the United States is required, among other things, to:

- Implement internal policies and procedures to promote accountability of inmates who perpetuate sexual violence within the correctional system.

- Provide immediate crisis intervention following victim disclosure or identification.

- Utilize technologies and other state-of-the-art equipment to enhance monitoring (eliminate blind spots) and reduce the opportunities for victimizations.

- Conduct specialized pre-service and in-service training programs for correctional staff.

What this means is if another inmate rapes you in prison, that inmate should be prosecuted for this crime and receive an appropriate sentence. You, as a rape victim, should receive immediate mental health counseling about the trauma you experienced, along with medical care for any injuries you received and medication to prevent sexually transmitted diseases and the prevention of pregnancy. Prisons are upgrading their monitoring systems to cover all areas of the prison with video cameras to prevent rape from happening, and prison employees must receive PREA training either before or after they are hired. Sexual contact between inmates and prison staff members is against the law in most states and all federal prisons. If a female inmate becomes pregnant in prison and claims that a male staff member is the father of the child, a DNA test will be performed.

PREA pretty much guarantees that you will not be "welcomed" to prison by being raped. There is a problem with PREA, however:

It costs a good deal of money to implement. This money must come from American taxpayers and be filtered down to every U.S. prison. This is not happening the way it was meant to. Federal grant money is needed to do more research on prison rape and how it can be eliminated. It is best that you know the facts about sex in prison instead of waiting for the government to intervene on your behalf. Someday, PREA will be a very big help to all inmates. But for now, let us see things as they really are.

### Consensual sex

When men and women are locked into a prison for long periods of time, they are going to want to have sex — a primary human drive — just as they are going to want to eat, breathe, and sleep. It naturally follows that sometimes there will be two male or female inmates who agree to have consensual sex with each other. Inmates are very often incredibly lonely, frightened, and hopeless about rejoining society. They use sex as a means of comfort, to ease their fear and loneliness, and at least find a bit of peace about being in prison. Inmates who are not by choice homosexual are often involved in a sexual relationship with another inmate because they have no other outlet for their sexual and social needs.

### Non-consensual sex

Rape in prison is an entirely different matter. If you could examine the psychological evaluations of rapists, you would find that although they enjoyed the sexual contact with their victim(s), their primary goal was obtaining power and control over another person. In a rape situation, the rapist is expressing his or her need to dominate and humiliate someone else. Sexual assault is defined as any contact between the sex organ of one person and the sex organ, mouth, or anus of another or inserting any object into the sex organ, mouth, or anus of another person by the use of threat or force.

---

"Within a matter of days, if not hours, an unofficial prison welcome committee sorts new arrivals into those who will fight being raped, those who will pay for not being raped, and those who will become punks. If you don't fight or pay up, you become somebody's 'baby' until they're bored with you and sell you to someone else."

*— A. L., Inmate, Montana*

---

Here are some facts you should know about prison rape among male and female inmates:

- Most male or female prison rapists do not see themselves as homosexual.

- Rape can happen to any inmate, regardless of age, race, or sexual orientation. Victims and offenders can be either heterosexual or homosexual.

- Sexual satisfaction is not the primary reason for their sexual attack.

- Many prison rapists believe they must continue to participate in gang rapes to avoid becoming rape victims themselves.

- Most prison rapists have suffered severe damage to their masculine or feminine self-esteem in the past.

If you look at the "prison proper" dictionary of slang terms in the Index of this book, you will see there are many terms that describe prison sex and those involved in it. For example, a "punk" is a male heterosexual inmate who has been forced into continual sex acts with another dominant male — or "wolf" — while a "fag" is an inmate who is naturally homosexual and does not feel forced into having sex with other males.

This is the common profile of male prison rapists:

- They are generally between 20 to 30 years old.

- They are larger and stronger than their victims.

- They have almost always been convicted of crimes of violence.

- They feel more at home in a prison environment because of their natural tendencies toward violence.

- They are often gang members who are well-connected in the inmate gang hierarchy among those who have committed violent crimes.

Conversely, here is the profile of the typical male rape victims:

- Young, white first offenders who are physically small

- Physically weak

- Feminine characteristics, such as a high voice

- Unassertive, passive, and shy

- Not "street smart"

- May have been convicted of a sex crime against a child

Inmates who experience being raped have deep emotional scars that continue long after the rape is over. They live in fear of being raped again and often turn to self-destructive acts such as cutting themselves, becoming aggressive, or doing drugs in prison. Feelings of embarrassment, anger, guilt, panic, depression, and fear can continue for months or even years after an inmate has been raped. Sometimes they feel such rage about being raped that they kill their rapist. The Human Rights Watch (**www.hrw. org**) researchers recommend that prison officials take better precautions with potential rape targets, such as being more selective about assigning cell mates or not double-celling these inmates at all.

Most important to you, of course, is learning the problems that come from consensual sex with other inmates and also how you can protect yourself against being raped in prison. Here is what you need to know:

- The number of male inmates who have HIV or AIDS is increasing every year. Many inmates who were drug users that shared needles may not only have these diseases, but may also have hepatitis C, an incurable disease that eventually results in liver failure and death. If you have a consensual sexual relationship with another inmate, you risk contracting these deadly diseases that are transmitted by semen, blood, and other bodily fluids. Condoms are not given to prison inmates. Some inmates will do the right thing and tell you that they have these diseases, and some will not. If you are scared, lonely, and need comfort from others, there are other ways of easing your emotional pain.

- During your initial orientation while you are being processed into prison, listen very closely to what you are told about keeping yourself safe from being raped, and make sure you follow these instructions.

- Be aware of situations that make you feel uneasy. Trust your instincts. If it feels uncomfortable, get yourself away from the situation immediately.

- Never go into an unmonitored area or an off-limits area. Prison rapes happen when the victim is alone and there are no cameras or COs present. Keep yourself in full view of camera monitors and COs and other staff members. If you find yourself being forced into one of these areas, fight back and scream as loudly as you can. Call attention to yourself and your situation. COs know when and how rapes happen, and they will come to your aid. Even if your attacker threatens you to stay quiet, yell out anyway.

- If you believe that you are in danger of being raped, tell a CO or your unit manager. This is a time when snitching is in your best interest. You can be moved into a single cell unit or into protective segregation. The COs will watch you more closely to protect you from harm; they will not let others know that you asked for help from them, so you need not fear being retaliated against for snitching.

- Be sure to follow every one of the prison's rules. If you are known as a well-behaved inmate, the staff will take you more seriously if you go to them with your fears about being raped.

- Even if you are a first offender in prison, act in an assertive manner — but do not try to act overly tough. This could backfire on you. Carry yourself with confidence. Let the word get out that you will fight back against a rapist and that you will not participate in the rape of another inmate.

- Never accept commissary items as gifts from other inmates, or any other gift or special favor for that matter. This places you in debt to other inmates, and their price for repayment could very well be sexual contact with you.

- Avoid talking about sex with other inmates or being either nude or partially clothed in front of them, if you can help it. Other inmates may see this as a "come-on" or an interest in a sexual relationship.

- If you believe that your prison is not doing enough to keep inmates from being raped, this would be a good time to be a "squeaky wheel" and call attention to the problem. Sometimes the quickest way to get public officials to do the right thing is to shine the light on what they are not doing. The Eighth Amendment of the U.S. Constitution guarantees your right against cruel and unusual punishment. This includes your right to a safe environment. Make some noise. Send letters to newspapers, state representatives and senators, the Human Rights Watch, the American Civil Liberties Union (ACLU), and any other group that comes to mind. If other inmates know you will report a rape — yours or another inmate's — to the prison staff, you are less likely to be targeted and victimized.

## THE AMERICAN CIVIL LIBERTIES UNION

The ACLU was established in 1920 to promote the protection of all Americans from the violation of their constitutional rights. Among its staff members, most are attorneys who represent clients without charge. Often, an ACLU attorney focuses on violations of the First Amendment, including your right to freedom of religion, separation of church and state, due process under the law in criminal and civil cases, and your right to privacy. The ACLU also supports decriminalizing the use of heroin, cocaine, and marijuana. The ACLU frequently seeks to protect the constitutional rights of Neo-Nazi groups and the American Atheist Association. In contrast, the ACLU has fought to uphold a woman's right to abortion in the case of *Roe v. Wade* and supported the end of racial segregation in the 1954 case of *Brown v. Board of Education*. The ACLU is very visible in cases concerning the constitutional rights of inmates. Most recently, the group has filed suit against the Montana Board of Corrections on behalf of an inmate who alleged that his Eighth Amendment rights against cruel and unusual punishment were violated when he was placed in segregation. The ACLU often works with similar groups such as the Human Rights Watch, the Second Amendment Foundation, the American Liberty Association, and the National Center for Lesbian Rights. The ACLU's headquarters is located in New York. If you believe your civil rights have been violated, you can reach them via the Internet. Visit **www.aclu.org/affiliates** to find the nearest affiliate in your area.

## Check Your Understanding No. 12

1. True or False:   All alcohol in prison comes from "outside."

2. True or False:   Decongestants are the only drugs abused by inmates.

3. True or False:   PREA legislation prevents all forms of prison rape.

4. True or False:   Rape is mostly an act of power, not just a sex act.

5. True or False:   The best way to prevent yourself from being sexually assaulted is to know and follow all prison rules about safety.

# RACISM AND HATRED

Racism and hatred exist in prison just as they do on the streets, except it is on a much larger, deeper scale in prison. Inmates are not incarcerated for acts of kindness, but for violence, hate toward a victim, the use of drugs and alcohol, breaking society's rules, and criminally reckless behavior. We have already seen how gangs, both in and out of prison, form around race or ethnic backgrounds. This is certainly a form of racism. Racism leads to hatred, and hatred leads to violence.

While you prepare to go to prison, do some serious soul-searching about what kind of family you had and what part of the country you come from. For example, if you are white and you were born and raised in a small Ohio town, you may have never seen a Native American. But if you were raised in Oklahoma, home of the Cherokee Nation, Native Americans are a common sight. To African Americans raised in South Central Los Angeles, Asian inmates are a bit of a culture shock. Consider your own racial and ethnic background, and then prepare yourself to meet inmates who look different from you, speak differently, worship a different higher power, and have different values and behaviors from yours. You must learn to tolerate those who are not like you in many ways if you want to stay safe in prison and do your time as quickly as possible. Most of all, be prepared for racist attitudes from some inmates. These are some very powerful feelings, and they lead to many conflicts between inmates, or among inmates and correctional officers or other staff members. If you go into prison expecting that other inmates and staff members will look, think, feel and behave like you, this will definitely be a problem for you. You need not join a prison gang that matches your race, religion, or ethnic background; just be aware that prison populations are very diverse and that you should try to at least make peace with everyone whether you like them or not.

One reason African Americans are angry and bitter about being in prison is that a large percentage of their race are inmates, compared to Caucasian or Asian racial groups. Looking back all the way to colonial America, huge numbers of Africans were taken from their homeland and enslaved or murdered. Caucasians outnumber blacks in America, but in prison, black inmates outnumber Caucasians in a four-to-one ratio.

As you are reading this, ask yourself if you tend to be an angry person. If so, you will probably greatly increase that anger in prison until it turns in to hatred. You will be angry all the time, and you will learn to hate other races, religions, and anyone who is different from you. You will learn to hate the correctional officers who enforce the prison rules. You will learn to hate the doctors who do not give you the exact type of medical care you want. You will learn to hate prison food because you are not given just what you want to eat. You will learn to hate the prison routine.

Most of all, you will learn to hate yourself for being in prison. This attitude will not help you get out of prison safely and quickly. It will keep you in prison longer because your learned hatred will cause you to rack up disciplinary actions and you will not be inclined to better yourself through the prison's rehabilitation programs. It is easy to hate in prison. It is not easy to maintain your peace of mind and increase your chances for release on parole. Before you go to prison, think this over and make your choice about learned hatred because your future depends on the course of action you choose.

## CORRECTIONS OFFICERS

Corrections officers represent the other side of prison society. Before massive prison reforms that began in the mid-1900s, guards were nearly always white men, had only high school educations, and received no special training to work in prisons alongside inmates. Guards ruled their prisons with an iron hand, frequently using physical violence to subdue or punish unruly inmates. The federal prison that once sat on Alcatraz Island off the coast of San Francisco was home to America's most violent murderers and gangsters, including Al Capone, George "Machine Gun" Kelley, Doc and Fred Barker, and Alvin "Creepy" Karpis. Escape-proof Alcatraz was a federal prison that also relied on the guards' abilities to maintain order among the most vicious criminals in the nation.

Times have changed, and so have prisons. Instead of guards, those who watch over inmates are called corrections officers. This clearly infers that today the focus of prison is rehabilitation, or correction of illegal behaviors that resulted in an inmate's incarceration. COs not only have the responsibilities to maintain custody and control in the prison and prevent escape, they are also responsible for monitoring visitors to prevent contraband from entering prison, searching inmates and their cells for weapons, and breaking up gang fights and riots, among many other duties. Unlike the old prison guards, COs are now both male and female and are highly trained professionals. COs usually have college degrees in criminal justice or a similar field of study and must attend a special training academy before they begin their duties. Most state DOCs require that COs pass a civil service exam before they are job- or promotion-eligible. In addition, many states require potential COs to go through a psychological screening to prevent people who have unsuitable personality characteristics from becoming COs. The American Correctional Association Code of Ethics is located at **www.aca.org**. You will find that COs are held to very strict standards of behavior.

When you arrive at prison, the people you will meet first are the COs. They will conduct your orientation program, serve as your escorts to your meetings with the A&E team, and answer all your questions about prison rules and required behavior. It is in your best interests that you treat COs with respect at all times, but especially when you first arrive because you will be making an impression on the COs about who you are and how you will most likely act in prison. Will you be a troublemaker, or will you just do your time as quickly and quietly as possible? This is the first question the COs will ask themselves about you.

To get along well with the COs, refer to them as "sir" or "ma'am," "Officer," or by their name, such as "CO Jones." If you need something, ask rather than demand. You do not need to suck up to the COs; just be polite, courteous, and respectful, and this is the way you will be treated in return. A sincere "thank you" to a CO goes a long way. Some of your COs will be women. Treat them exactly as you treat male COs. Do not treat a female CO in a sexual or disrespectful manner; this will earn you a serious disciplinary report, and the parole board will not like it either.

When the COs ask you to do something, just do it. Do not ask why or argue about it. These people have an entire cell block to oversee and cannot waste time engaging in a meaningless argument with you over a rule or procedure. In their training academy, COs are taught to disengage themselves from too much conversation with inmates, to not get involved in inmates' affairs, and to stay emotionally detached from inmates. You may feel that prison life is stressful — COs have the same feelings.

Keep in mind that just because the COs have no desire to be your friend does not mean that they care nothing about you. On the contrary, COs really do want you to be rehabilitated. This includes learning to follow rules and obey authority figures. If you show that you can do this in prison, you can convince the parole board that you can obey laws on the outside. Your official prison file will contain information written by COs: things you have done correctly as well as problems you have caused. Prison overcrowding is a serious problem in America, so every additional inmate means one more person for the COs to manage. The more inmates who "make good" on parole and do not return to prison, the easier the CO's job becomes.

Just as inmates have a "convict's code," there is also an unwritten "CO code" that can be summarized below:

- Always help another CO in maintaining control and custody.

- Do not allow contraband to be brought into the prison.

- Do not "rat" on another CO who is making a mistake.

- Never make another CO look bad in front of inmates.

- Always support a CO in a dispute with an inmate.

- Always support another CO's disciplinary write-up of an inmate.

- Maintain CO solidarity versus other groups on the inside.

- Express concern for other COs in a helpful manner.

## DO CORRECTIONS OFFICERS SOMETIMES SIDE WITH THE INMATES?

Yes. In 1994, eight COs at the Corcoran State Prison in California were indicted in a federal court on charges of violating the civil rights of inmates. The "Corcoran Eight" were accused of staging fights between rival gang inmates in the recreation yard and betting on the outcome. A CO killed one inmate in the guard tower during an inmate fight. It was the report of two other COs that prompted an intensive investigation of Corcoran's CO staff. These two COs were constantly harassed and threatened by other COs at Corcoran and other prisons. They eventually retired and won a million-dollar lawsuit because officials at Corcoran failed to protect them under federal "whistleblower" laws. The Corcoran Eight faced possible lengthy prison sentences. All eight were found not guilty of the charges against them. Since that time, there have been no more reports of serious misconduct by COs at Corcoran.

## COs aren't the enemy

If you do your time without making a CO's job even harder, you will find that the COs are the first staff members who will speak positively of you with the parole board. Avoiding common mistakes and poor decisions while you are in prison will help you serve your time and make parole. Unlike many new inmates, you have this book to help you understand in advance the mistakes and decisions that could cost you your parole. We can use Tom's case as an example of this issue.

## HOW YOU ACT IN PRISON IS AN INDICATOR OF HOW YOU WILL ACT IN SOCIETY

Tom and Randy both attend a group discussion on rehabilitation and criminal thinking three times a week with Jane, a mental health counselor. During one session, Jane asked the group what they had learned about common mistakes and poor decisions that some inmates make.

"I'm asking you this," said Jane, "because if you can recognize errors in thinking while you are in prison, you should be able to do this on the outside when you are paroled. How you act in prison is an indicator of how you will act in society. Your manner of thinking on the outside is what got you to prison; if you want out, you need to change the way you think."

Randy, who was nearing his parole board hearing, said, "I make mistakes when I act on impulse. I do not think things through, like what could go wrong and what my consequences might be. I just do stuff because, at the time, I feel like it."

Jane asked, "How did this type of thinking work for you?"

"It didn't," said Randy. "That's why I'm in here."

Derek, another inmate, said, "There's nothin' wrong 'bout my thinking. The white boys just want all us brothers in prison so they don't have to deal with us."

Tom said, "Man, you don't get it. You've been kicked out of the world. We all have. Now *this* is our world, and I want out."

Jane said, "Tom, you recently had a disciplinary write-up for being disrespectful to a medical staff member. Do you want to talk about it?"

Tom replied, "I was tired and pissed off that day. I kept thinking about wanting to go home. I felt bad about the girl I hurt. It was a really bad day, and when Dr. Jensen said I couldn't keep my headache medicine in my cell, I got frustrated and called him a bald (expletive). He wrote me up and I went to the hole for three days so I could adjust my attitude." Jane said, "So you took your anger out on another person."

"Yeah," Tom said. "Before I came here, I would have had a few drinks and just gone numb if I was feeling bad. Here, I can't do that, so I just got mad and ran my mouth."

Sanchez, another inmate, said, "I did the same crap; I was pissed all the time and in and out of the hole. This cost me my first parole. No more, dude. You gotta find another, better way to be angry without being a jerk."

## COMMON MISTAKES INMATES MAKE

These are some of the most common mistakes and errors in thinking that inmates make in prison:

- Needing instant gratification — you want what you want when you want it.

- Failure to think about the consequences of your actions.

- Using others as targets for your negative emotions, such as anger and frustration.

- Not learning from past mistakes.

- Failure to be aware that your behavior is always the result of your thoughts.

- Having "core beliefs" about yourself and your environment that cause you problems, such as, "Nobody can order me around," "I'm better than those people," and, "People will always take advantage of you, especially in prison. So I'll get them first."

- "Extreme" thinking — all or nothing — leads to poor choices and decisions. For example, "I hate all white people," or, "I'll get what I want, or else."

- "Personalization" means that everything is about you. For example, "He bumped into me because he disrespects me," or, "CO Jones locked the unit down because he wants to punish me." As TV's favorite psychologist, Dr. Phil says, "It ain't about you."

- Jumping to conclusions is a common mistake that leads you to make snap decisions that have no basis in fact. For example, "Larry's high on something; the doc must have slipped it to him because Larry's his pet," or "What's that dude looking at me for? He must think I'm a punk. I'll knock the crap out of him right now!"

- Rigid, concrete thinking can lead to poor choices that could hurt you in the long run. For example, "My mama said I was stupid, so I cannot learn to read," or, "Everybody in my family smokes weed, so I will too," and "I'm just a loser; I'm no good."

These are just a few of the mental errors that can lead you to make poor choices and decisions while you are in prison. Remember, if you make these mistakes on the inside, you are going to make them on the outside, too.

It is time to check your understanding about this material.

## Check Your Understanding No. 13

1. True or False:    Corrections officers today have no formal training in their jobs.

2. True or False:    Just being polite and respectful will help you get along with COs.

3. True or False:    Extreme thinking can lead to poor choices and decisions.

4. True or False:    Learning racism and hatred will not help you be released from prison.

5. True or False:    Thinking about your own background can help you become more tolerant of people who are different from you.

# PRIVACY IN PRISON

Privacy in prison is difficult — if not impossible — to come by, so do not expect any. The reason for this is simple: Monitoring the prison for custody and control means personal privacy is lost. You must prepare yourself to have the mind-set that staff members, usually COs, are monitoring everything you do. In most prison cell blocks, there is a "cage" that is bulletproof, shatterproof, and electronically sealed. Only the cage CO can open and shut doors on the block or unit. The cage has mounted camera monitors that continuously provide visual views of every part of the prison where inmates are allowed to go. The cage officer can immediately alert a nearby CO if a conflict or rule violation occurs in the block. You must be prepared to eat, drink, shower, visit with friends and family, watch TV, read in your cell, play cards in the common room, or go to the commissary, recreation yard, gym, group therapy, and infirmary, all while being watched by a video camera and cage CO. Your cell contains a sink and toilet. If you need to brush your teeth or relieve yourself on the toilet, you will most likely be in full view of other inmates and staff.

Federal courts have decreed that inmates have no right to privacy. Thus, COs can, at any time, search your body and your cell. From a simple pat-down search to a full body cavity search, a CO has the right to examine you for any type of contraband. When your cell is searched, this is called a shakedown. A "universal key" can unlock any cell, and the cage CO can open electronic locks. In our civilian society, police officers cannot enter our homes and look through our belongings without a search warrant signed by a judge. In prison, COs can conduct a shakedown any time they wish. Be prepared to have your books and magazines examined, your hygiene items tasted or smelled, your bed stripped and searched, your clothing examined, and every inch of your cell's walls and floors inspected. A shakedown can take place in one inmate's cell, or in an entire cell block or unit. If contraband is found, the inmate who had it is seriously disciplined by spending up to 90 days in segregation and losing several privileges such as going to the commissary or the recreation yard. Contrary to Hollywood stereotypes, COs do not like to do shakedowns because they are difficult and extremely time-consuming. The unit is usually in lockdown status during a shakedown, which means that no one goes anywhere until the shakedown is complete.

As you prepare to go to prison, keep in mind that there is nothing you can do to regain your privacy or prevent body searches and shakedowns. As long as you are not in possession of contraband, you have nothing to fear from these searches. You will not like it, but you will get used to using the toilet and showering in full view of others. Remember that these are security measures by the prison that may someday save your life.

# 6 | Medical Care in Prison

In previous chapters, you learned a bit about the medical care you will receive in prison. This chapter goes into much more detail so you can feel secure about your medical care as you are preparing to go to prison. Remember, it is your responsibility to make sure you bring all of your medical records with you, or have them sent directly to the prison.

---

"When I see a patient, I don't want to deal with a whole laundry list of his medical concerns. At each appointment, I want to deal with one issue at a time. Today we might discuss his acid reflux condition; at his next appointment is the time to discuss his sinus headaches. Doing it this way is the only way for a physician to manage so many inmates' medical care."

— *T.K., Prison Physician*

---

# MEET YOUR PHYSICIAN

First, we should examine the role of your physician. He or she will evaluate your health and provide treatment for your medical needs. Your prison will be staffed with between one and three physicians, depending on the size and population of the facility. Your physician — it is usually fine to call him or her "Doc" — is an employee of your state's DOC and is most often an expert in practicing medicine in a correctional facility.

## CAN YOU FIRE YOUR PHYSICIAN IN PRISON?

No, you cannot. Nor can your doctor fire you as a patient. The reality of correctional medicine is that an inmate and a doctor are stuck with each other. Some prisons have only one physician. Conflicts between inmates and their doctors can most often be resolved through good communication and understanding each other's position on medical care. However, if you believe you are receiving inadequate or incompetent medical care, you can file a complaint about this with the warden.

In some prisons, physicians are dressed similar to COs, complete with badges and handcuffs. They may also be trained and licensed to use firearms but do not carry a weapon on the job. Most physicians in correctional settings discourage this practice; they prefer to wear normal business clothes and white coats so you can feel more comfortable with them. You should be able to speak freely with your physician about your health care and trust that he or she has your best interest at heart.

Below are some of the problems associated with medicine in a correctional facility:

- Security precautions often conflict with patient care and the physician/patient relationship. For example, male and female inmates in maximum-security units are brought to medical appointments in arm, waist, and leg shackles. This makes a physical examination of inmates rather difficult for the physician. Security overrides all other issues.

- Also with maximum-security inmates, at least one corrections officer is present during the inmate's medical appointment. Female COs are assigned this duty for a female patient. Confidentiality between doctor and patient is sometimes limited if an inmate's sensitive medical issues are heard by another person. Of course, COs are trained to maintain an inmate's confidentiality; it is a violation of ethics and prison rules for a CO to discuss an inmate's medical issues with another person except on an emergency basis.

- Prison overcrowding in America is a serious issue in all aspects of prison life, including when it comes to your medical care. Your state prison may have only limited funds to hire competent medical personnel; the saying "you get what you pay for" applies in this instance. DOCs must pay top-notch physicians what they would earn if they were practicing medicine on the outside. Doctors make good money because they are worth it. If only low pay is offered, few — if any — competent physicians will want to work in correctional medicine. With overcrowding, your prison physician has only a limited amount of time to spend with you. This is not because he or she does not care about you, but because your doctor may have 25 more patients to see that day.

- Your doctor has only limited resources within the prison infirmary. This applies to medications, diagnostic procedures like MRIs, and devices like crutches and wheelchairs. Again, security plays a part here, too, when you consider that crutches and similar items can be used as weapons. If you seriously need a medication that is not stocked in the infirmary, your physician will submit a request to obtain this medication for you only if no other medication in the prison infirmary will do the job.

- There are some medications that you will be allowed to keep in your cell or in your pocket. You will have to come to the infirmary for pill pass for any other medications. Do not complain to your physician about this. The doctor is following the rules of the prison, just as you must.

- Your physician has the final word about your medical care. According to the U.S. Supreme Court case *Estelle v. Gamble,* your doctor must provide you with *adequate* medical care, not necessarily the kind of care you want. The Eighth Amendment to the U.S. Constitution protects inmates from cruel and unusual punishment. This includes providing sub-standard medical care, or no care at all. According to this case, you would have to prove that your physician acted with intentional "depraved indifference" to your health care needs simply because you are a convicted criminal.

- You have the right to refuse medical and/or mental health care in prison, just as a non-incarcerated person does. This includes refusing to take prescribed medications even though they have been deemed essential for your quality of life and may actually save your life. For example, you can refuse to take medicine for high blood pressure even though not taking it may cause you to have a stroke that could result in your death. You also have the right to refuse measures that prolong your life even though you have no brain activity. This can be done through a "do not resuscitate" (DNR) document or a "living will" document; you can find these forms online or ask your attorney to prepare them for you.

If you need to schedule an appointment to see your prison physician, you will need to fill out a request form usually called a "kite," though each prison has its own name for this form. To properly complete your kite, you must state the reason you need to see the doctor. In addition to routine medical care, you can use a kite to request temporary leave from your prison work assignment for a legitimate medical reason.

## SPECIAL MEDICAL NEEDS

If you have special medical needs, you can use a kite to begin the process of having your physician help you with those needs, such as:

- **Housing needs:** If you have difficulty getting to the top bunk in your cell or you could fall out of the bunk, your physician can give you a "low bunk" pass. These passes are often given for medical conditions such as epilepsy, confinement to a wheelchair, blindness in one or both eyes, amputations, obesity, and severe orthopedic conditions like arthritis.

- **Bedding needs:** If you need an extra pillow or mattress, your physician can arrange this for a special medical need such as gastric reflux disease, chronic back pain, or an injury to your arms or legs.

- **Shoe needs:** If you have a foot problem such as a foot deformity, your physician can arrange for you to wear only soft-soled shoes like sneakers. You may need shoe sole inserts if you have diabetes, very flat feet, or foot ulcers or sores.

- **Medical appliances:** Your physician can arrange for you to have a cane, crutches, slings, wheelchairs, oxygen tanks, an insulin pump, or a CPAP machine for nighttime oxygen provision. In these cases, your physician must work with security personnel because medical appliances can also be used as weapons. If you have a history of violent behavior, correctional medicine physicians have a duty to find an alternative to the use of these devices if at all possible. If no alternative is possible, you will be given the device you need, but your security and custody level may be changed to "maximum."

- Other types of medical "passes" include not being required to wear handcuffs behind your back, being able to walk slowly due to a handicap or being elderly, and being able to eat slowly.

# THE ATHENS OATH

To dispel many of the myths and stereotypes about correctional physicians, you may find the "Athens Oath" interesting. This oath originated from a group of prison physicians in Athens, Georgia, and it was presented at the 1977 World Congress of Prison Medicine. The Athens Oath is very specific in its intent: "We recognize the right for incarcerated individuals to receive the best possible medical care." Before you were convicted of a crime, you expected your doctor to be attentive to all your medical needs and provide you with necessary medications, medical tests, and even surgical procedures when necessary. Now that you have become an inmate, correctional physicians will provide you with the same type of care. Under the Athens Oath, your doctor does not care about the nature of the crime you committed; many times he or she does not even know this information because it is usually not relevant to your medical care. The Athens Oath has five basic, easy principles:

1.   Correctional physicians will not authorize or approve of any type of physical punishment of inmates.

2.   Correctional physicians will not participate in any form of the torture of inmates.

3.   Correctional physicians will respect the confidentiality of medical information told to them by inmates.

4.   Correctional physicians will not engage in any form of human experimentation among inmates without their informed consent.

5.    Correctional physicians will make medical judgments based upon the needs of inmates and take priority over any non-medical matters.

## *The case that changed prison medical care*

In 1976, the Supreme Court's ruling in the case of *Estelle v. Gamble* prevented prison physicians from engaging in "deliberate indifference" of inmates' medical needs. This became the law of the land, and the case continues to uphold your constitutional right against cruel and unusual punishment in prison. In 2005, a number of inmates successfully sued the California Department of Corrections because of deliberate indifference by the prison physicians. In this case, *Plata v. Schwarzenegger*, U.S. District Judge Thelton Henderson wrote that in a review of cases where 193 prison deaths occurred, medical records in 34 of these cases were either lost or found to be "highly problematic, with multiple instances of incompetence, indifference, neglect, and even cruelty by the medical staff."

What these legal cases mean to you, as an inmate, is that the eyes of the nation are focused upon the type of medical care that you will receive in prison. The "bad old days" included inmates being denied competent medical care, and no national standards of correctional medical care existed in America. Today's prison medical staff must be sure to address such things as:

- The competency and caring manner of each member of the medical staff

- Infirmary care and special medical care that is available within the community

- Maintaining complete medical records for each inmate

- The interaction between the medical staff and security personnel

- Care of the terminally ill inmates

- Care of inmates' infectious diseases such as HIV/AIDS, hepatitis C, and tuberculosis

- Care of mentally ill inmates

- Care of pregnant inmates

- Protecting an inmate's confidentiality to the degree possible in a prison setting

- The treatment of pain within a prison setting

Also note the following requirements:

- Disciplinary action such as segregation should not cause the denial of medical care.

- In keeping with their medical oaths, correctional physicians must not be required to participate in the execution of an inmate.

- Prisons should have mandatory quality care standards, and physicians' records should be reviewed to make sure they are following these standards.

- Prisons should have the ability to care for the elderly and the terminally ill inmate.

Tom's case provides us with an illustration of these points:

## RESPECT THOSE WHO ARE TRYING TO HELP YOU

Tom returned from a medical appointment, and Randy thought that he was angry about something. Tom said, "Dr. Shore doesn't listen to anything I say. I tried to talk with him about my long history of really bad headaches and I asked him to prescribe me some sedatives. When my head hurts, the only thing that helps is if I go to sleep for a long time. My doc on the outside prescribed them, so why can't I get them here?"

Randy said, "Did you ask him what the problem is?"

Tom responded, "No, not really. I guess I was pretty angry when he said no. I tried to convince him but he kept on saying no." An inmate named Michael overhead their conversation and approached Tom.

"Dude, those docs don't care about any of us cons. We're just human garbage to them." Michael gave Tom a copy of the court case *Estelle v. Gamble* and told Tom that he should contact a lawyer about "depraved indifference" in his medical care. He said, "That (expletive) Shore, he don't give you nothing. He's just here to get an easy paycheck."

Later that day, Tom received a disciplinary write-up from the unit CO for using profanity with Dr. Shore. The complaint stated that during his medical appointment, Tom could be heard shouting, arguing, and calling Dr. Shore a "dumb mother (expletive)." Tom stormed out of the doctor's office and said to his escorting CO, "get me the (expletive) out of here. I want to go back to my cell where at least somebody gives a (expletive) about me." Tom admitted that he had said those things and that he was very frustrated and angry at the time and felt like hitting somebody. Since he was still very angry when the CO asked him about the write-up, Tom was transferred to segregation for three days where he had no privileges and could not leave his cell. Tom cooled off during this time and told the unit CO that he would like to talk with Dr. Shore again about his head-aches, and that he would calmly listen to the doctor and ask questions respectfully.

Dr. Shore agreed and explained to Tom that the use of powerful seda-tives for Tom's migraine-type headaches was not only old-fashioned, but not used anymore since the triptan class of medications became available. He said that the prison pharmacy stocked Imitrex®, one of those medications that works very well on migraines by constricting the inflamed blood vessels in the brain that cause migraines. This drug, unlike sedatives, is not addictive and usually produces very good results within a couple of hours. "Your headaches will be treated, not just drugged," Dr. Shore told Tom. "You'll need to lie down for a while, but after that, you'll be up and around, feeling much better."

Tom nodded but didn't know what to say. He thought about the court case that Morgan had given him. Dr. Shore said, "I really do care about you, Tom. I care about all my patients. I want to give you the very best, most modern treatment possible. Will you send me a kite right away the next time you get a migraine headache?" Tom said that yes, he would like to try this new medication. Tom apologized to Dr. Shore for becom-ing so angry and using profanity with him. Dr. Shore shook Tom's hand and said, "I understand, but I don't want you to speak to me like that. I treat you respectfully, and I ask that you show me the same courtesy, okay?"

Tom's conflict with Dr. Shore was easily solved when Tom became calm and listened to Dr. Shore rather than shouting profanity at him because he did not get what he wanted. Tom's case is an example of what not to do during a medical appointment. It is clear that Dr. Shore's medical care with Tom did not constitute the "depraved indifference" described by *Estelle v. Gamble*.

To sum up the type of medical care you will receive in prison, remember these two points: (1) Inmates should be treated with respect, not neglect, and (2) inmates should have the same quality of care as that given to non-inmates.

Let us check your understanding of the material presented in this section.

## Check Your Understanding No. 14

1. True or False:   One of the main challenges in prison medicine is overcrowding.

2. True or False:   You cannot fire your prison physician.

3. True or False:   Court cases have failed to review the medical care of inmates.

4. True or False:   A kite is a form inmates use to request a medical appointment.

5. True or False:   The Athens Oath was designed to ensure adequate medical for inmates.

# END-OF-LIFE ISSUES

"End-of-life" issues may refer to patients who are deemed critically ill and may want to end treatment in order to receive their "right to die." Your prison's administration and medical staff must consider these issues. Your prison will have special policies and procedures for the elderly, the terminally ill, and those facing the death penalty. Not only is this simply the right, moral thing to do, but you must also take into account that more inmates are dying in prison today because of non-parole or lengthy sentences, a rising number of inmates with alcohol and other drug-related illnesses, and increased violence among inmates that can result in death.

## Compassionate release

Compassionate release is when an inmate is facing imminent death and wishes to die among friends and family members. The inmate is released on a special type of parole. If compassionate release is granted, the parole board has decided that the dying inmate is no longer a threat to society. This type of release is controversial.

## A dying inmate's last wish

Susan Atkins has served 37 years in prison. This is the longest time served by any woman in America. Atkins was charged with being directly involved in the 1969 Charles Manson "Family" murders of seven people in Los Angeles. Per Manson's orders, Susan and three other family members broke into the home of actress Sharon Tate and director Roman Polanski to kill everyone in the home. Atkins herself stabbed Sharon Tate to death, who was nine months pregnant at the time. Sharon begged for the life of her child; Atkins admitted, "I told her I didn't have mercy for her." Atkins was also convicted in an earlier murder of music teacher Gary Hinman. Atkins, Manson, and the other killers were sentenced to death, but California later abolished the death penalty, and instead their sentences were all commuted to life inprisonment.

At age 61, Susan was suffering from terminal brain cancer, with one leg amputated and the other leg paralyzed. According to her physicians, she had only a few months to live. In July 2008, a parole board denied her request for compassionate release but gave no explanation for its decision — it is not required to do so. Susan's niece, Sharisse Atkins, 17 at the time, told the press, "She has without a doubt paid her debt to society. You see her as a part of the Manson family, I see her as a part of our family. I hope you can find it in your heart to do the right thing."

Manson prosecutor Vincent Bugliosi supported Atkins' release. In an e-mail to Atkins' attorney, Bugliosi wrote that it was wrong to say "just because Susan Atkins showed no mercy to her victims, we therefore are duty-bound to follow her inhumanity and show no mercy to her." Bugliosi had, until that point in time, been vehemently opposed to the parole of any of the Manson killers. While in prison, Susan married a man who lives in Orange County, California, who joined in her request for compassionate release.

Those opposed to Susan's release were many, including the relatives of the Manson Family murder victims, the current Los Angeles District Attorney, the Orange County District Attorney, and the Director of California Prisons. In addition to testimony by Atkins and others, the parole board also had her medical records, recommendations regarding her release by corrections officials, documentation of her behavior in prison, and collected information about whether her compassionate release would pose a danger to society.

Atkins' parole was denied for a 13th time on September 2, 2009. Hearing officials cited the "atrocious" and "dispassionate" nature of the murders she committed. Shortly after being denied parole one last time, Atkins died at the Central California Women's Facility in Chowchilla.

## Hospice care in prison

In addition to compassionate release, many states have a hospice program for terminally ill prisoners. In this type of program, a dying inmate is transferred to a home-like setting in a community to spend his or her last days. Those who support hospice programs maintain that their residents are too ill to be a risk to society and wish only to die with dignity rather than in a prison infirmary. Correctional experts also show that hospice care for terminally ill inmates is much less expensive that prison or community hospital care. The National Prison Hospice Association (NPHA) was formed in 1991 to provide information and recommendations regarding hospice care for terminally ill inmates.

Correctional medicine focuses on the necessity of providing humane, skilled medical care for inmates in their final days. When you enter your prison, you may see that some inmates are housed in a special area. This is because they have infectious diseases such as HIV/AIDS or hepatitis B or C. Being housed in such a unit is not a punishment of any kind; it is only a precaution to keep infectious diseases from spreading within the prison. Within the past two decades, the number of male and female inmates with these illnesses has greatly increased.

You may also meet a number of elderly inmates. These inmates are provided the medication and medical appliances they need by your infirmary staff. Prison physicians are skilled in treating Alzheimer's disease, diabetes, eyesight and hearing problems, and other issues common among the elderly. We can use Tom's case as an example of how old age is managed in prison.

## HELPING THOSE WHO ARE AGING IN PRISON

Tom and Randy's cell was located next door to Deke and Marshall's cell. Deke was 73 years old and serving a life sentence for homicide. Marshall told Tom that Deke had problems walking due to severe arthritis in his knees, and that Deke's physician recommended that he have a wheelchair. Deke, said Marshall, wanted the wheelchair but did not think he had the strength in his arms to push himself.

Marshall said that because his work program was outside the prison, he would not be around to push Deke. Later, Randy told Tom that volunteering to be a wheelchair "pusher" would be a good thing for both Deke and Tom. Deke liked Tom because they always had a joke to tell each other, and Tom would have this volunteer service on his record when he met the parole board. Tom agreed, and the following day he told Deke that he would be his pusher and help him get wherever he needed to go. The next week, Deke had his wheelchair; Tom pushed him to medical appointments, to the chow hall, to church services, to see his son when he visited, and to the library.

# ALCOHOL AND DRUG TREATMENT IN PRISON

If you are in prison because of an alcohol or other drug-related offense, or if you had a drug problem before you committed the offense for which you were convicted, you will find that the prison offers rehabilitation that may be overseen by the medical or mental health staff. In fact, if you were convicted of a drug-related offense, unless you can verify your regular attendance in 12-step support programs, it is not likely that you will be paroled.

The board that denies your parole will usually insist that you begin attending support group meetings at once, before your next parole hearing.

The most common forms of substance abuse rehabilitation in prisons are the 12-step programs such as Alcoholics Anonymous and Narcotics Anonymous. It is very important for you to understand that 12-step programs are not medically supervised treatment programs, but are support group programs. In prison, the AA and NA programs are conducted and monitored by either a staff member who has, in the past, had drug or alcohol problems, or by AA or NA volunteers in the community who come to the prison especially to manage these programs. Inmates who are addicts and who regularly attend AA and NA meetings are often co-group leaders within these programs. In addition, prison chaplains often counsel inmates regarding alcohol and drugs. It is likely that your prison does not have a medically supervised treatment program. Such programs consist primarily of intensive individual and group therapy and medications for the depression that usually coexists with drug and/or alcohol addiction. Very up-to-date treatment programs can involve the use of a prescription medication called acamprosate that relieves the preoccupation and craving for alcohol.

While researchers have firmly established that an overwhelming number of crimes are tied to substance abuse, treatment programs and medications are expensive, and thinly stretched DOC budgets cannot afford either of them. In his book *Drugs, Society and Criminal Justice,* Charles Levinthal makes the case that both private and government studies are united in their findings that drug use, including alcohol, and crime are firmly linked, and that it is impossible to find a study that does not find that drugs and crime are related. You should always keep in mind that people who abuse alcohol and other drugs are more likely to commit crimes than people who do not. It stands to reason that if you get straight and stay straight while you are in prison, this will greatly increase your chances of never returning to prison.

Before you go to prison, you should know that there is currently a controversy over courts and parole boards making a 12-step program mandatory for inmates who apply for parole. This issue is twofold: the effectiveness of the programs, and their reliance on a higher power or supreme being. Because Alcoholics Anonymous and Narcotics Anonymous are obviously anonymous and no one but the group knows the names of those who attend these support programs, it is extremely difficult to know whether they are successful in the long term in keeping members abstinent from alcohol or drugs. There is an unsubstantiated theory that only 2 percent of AA members remain sober for the rest of their lives. Thus, the problem statement is something like this: "Why should we force inmates to attend AA or NA if we are not even sure that it works?" It is also not an issue of funding, since AA and NA volunteers do not charge for their services, and prison chaplains and mental health staff members are already receiving a salary for their work.

Then there is the issue of a dependence on a higher power or supreme being in these models. In most 12-step programs, members must admit that they are helpless and powerless over drugs and alcohol, and that only a higher power can "return them to sanity." A member's higher power is referred to as "God *as we understand Him.*" Although AA and NA claim not to be solely Christian-based and that all religions are welcome in their groups, most of these programs have Christian-oriented "prayers for the day" and use other books that quote the Christian Bible. Traditional 12-step programs adamantly deny having a Christian-based foundation; therefore, faith in Jesus Christ is not mentioned in their books or meetings.

Just as AA and other 12-step programs are coming under fire for their alleged ineffectiveness, they are also being challenged because of their required belief in a higher power. Inmates, parolees, and those on probation through the justice system are challenging a court or parole board's right to make them attend what they believe to be religion-oriented programs. An inmate who exercises his or her right to not believe in a higher power as guaranteed by the U.S. Constitution would be forced to attend a 12-step program against his or her wishes and beliefs.

Jack Trimpey, a licensed clinical social worker (LCSW), began a program called Rational Recovery in 1986. In RR, there is no helplessness or powerlessness, nor is there a reliance on any type of higher power required. There are no steps and no meetings, and there is no life-long dependence on attending such meetings as in AA and other 12-step programs. Trimpey believes that these programs are ineffective, border on religious cults, and develop lifelong dependency on the group instead of the abused substance. He wrote that this dependency is the most destructive type of rehabilitation in our country; we are a "12-step nation," instead of using our minds and willpower to recover from substance abuse and stay sober for life. Nor does Trimpey see addicts as "sick" as in the AA "medical disease" model. He says alcohol and other drug addictions result from the user making extremely bad and immoral decisions that negatively affect him and others. In his books, DVDs, seminars, and Internet forum, he breaks down the RR philosophy into one simple question: What is your plan for the future use of alcohol and/or drugs? In RR, a person's ability to make the Big Plan is all-important: "I will never drink (or use drugs) again, and I will never change my mind." That is it; no slogans, no meetings, and no steps.

When you arrive in prison, you may find that a 12-step program may be voluntary rather than mandatory, and that the study of RR and its sobriety principles is also available to you. You can begin your recovery by writing a kite to your physician, letting him or her know that you need help in recovery from substance abuse. You will then receive a referral to the mental health staff, who will help you determine what type of recovery program is right for you. Keep in mind our discussion of the presence of alcohol and other drugs in prison; do not assume that just because you are in prison you will not be tempted to use these substances. Also keep in mind that when you are released from prison, you may be even more tempted. If you are really serious about eliminating alcohol and/or drugs from your life, all the opportunities for staying sober are right there in prison for you.

Tom's case provides a meaningful explanation of this material.

## ALCOHOLICS ANONYMOUS MEETINGS

Because Tom's criminal offense was directly related to his addiction to alcohol, a staff mental health specialist recommended that he attend Alcoholics Anonymous three times a week. Tom had never been to AA but decided it was in his best interest to at least try it. The AA group met that evening; Angus, the inmate group leader, welcomed Tom by saying "Hello, Tom. I'm Angus, and I'm an alcoholic." As was their custom, the group reviewed the 12 steps and 12 traditions of Alcoholics Anonymous, and then each group member had an opportunity to speak about his or her destructive use of alcohol, how this resulted in being sent to prison, and how the AA program was helping him or her stay sober.

Angus said, "There's booze in prison. Anybody can sneak around and make pruno in his cell if it's worth a lot of time in lockdown. But if I can't stay sober in prison, I sure as hell won't stay sober on the outside where there's booze around every corner." Angus and other group members discussed feeling helpless to control their use of alcohol without the help of their personal "Higher Power." Angus explained to Tom that AA does not refer only to the Christian God, but to *God as you understand Him.* Tom was a little troubled by this, but he said nothing to Randy until after the meeting. "What if I'm not sure that I believe in God?" he said to Randy. "I never have been religious. I don't think I have to depend on some kind of God to keep me from drinking; I can do that myself if I honestly set my mind to it. I've never been tempted to look for any pruno since I've been in prison."

"Me neither, but I know it's here," said Randy. "Angus seems like a straight-up guy. Why don't you talk to him?"

The next day, Tom sat down with Angus after chow. Angus said, "Listen, AA is one way, but it isn't the only way to get sober and stay that way. It works for me, but it may not be your thing. What difference does it make as long as you're not drinking and hurting yourself and others?" He gave Tom pamphlets on Rational Recovery. After obtaining permission to use a computer in the study room, Angus showed Tom how to access the RR Web site at **http://rational.org**. Tom printed RR's history, principles, and information about using the material to keep sober.

Tom said, "Angus, thanks a lot. You don't know what it means to me to find a sobriety program that won't keep me in meetings for the rest of my life and believing that I can't control my own actions."

Narcotics Anonymous is a 12-step group based on the same principles as AA. This support group program is not always found in prisons, but you can obtain their books at the Web site for the Hazelden Foundation (**www.hazelden.org**), a not-for-profit alcohol and drug addiction treatment center with recovery services. If you cannot afford to buy the NA books, ask your doctor, your mental health counselor, or your chaplain about community-based NA groups that buy these books for inmates.

To end this chapter, check your understanding of the material in this section.

## Check Your Understanding No. 15

1. True or False:   Inmates can volunteer to help others with medical issues such as difficulty walking.

2. True or False:   Compassionate release for terminally ill inmates is always granted.

3. True or False:   The only types of alcohol and drug programs in prison today are 12-step programs.

4. True or False:   Elderly inmates rarely have their medical needs met.

5. True or False:   Medical treatment for alcohol and other drug abuse is found in most prisons.

# CHAPTER 7

## You and Your Family Before and During Your Incarceration

Some researchers claim that a strong family bond is the most important issue that determines whether a parolee will break the conditions of his parole and return to prison. Thus, we need to take a serious, reflective look at you and your family members' relationships and how you can remain emotionally close to them while you are in prison. Inmates with children are torn between these choices:

- I need to see my kids and be active in their lives. I need for them to know how much I love and miss them. I must show them that I will never abandon them.

- I do not want my children to see me like this. If they do, they will always have that picture in their minds of their "jailbird" mother or father. They will hate me for not being with them, and they will be embarrassed and ashamed of me. Maybe they will be better off without me.

Inmates without children may also feel these things about their partners and their parents. Since you have probably served time in jail prior to your trial and sentencing, you have had a glimpse of which loved ones want to keep a relationship with you while you are in prison and those who do not. Since this is their choice, you have no option but to abide by their decisions. In preparing your family for your period of incarceration, we can use Tom's case as an example.

## TOM'S FAMILY

Tom has a wife, Sandra, of eight years. He regards this as a permanent, committed relationship. He has two children, ages 4 and 6. While Tom was awaiting trial in the county jail, Sandra told him that both kids have asked several times where their daddy was and when he would come home. Sandra did not let their children visit Tom in jail. She felt it would confuse and frighten them. When Tom was about to be transferred to prison, he and Sandra decided they needed to make a plan for Tom's visitation with the children. First, Sandra told Tom that she would stay with him as his wife as long as his behavior in prison was good and he participated in alcohol abuse counseling.

She agreed to frequently visit Tom. Sandra, as the legal custodian of the children, would make the decisions about the children visiting Tom in prison. Tom discussed this issue with his mental health counselor, and then he told Sandra that he would like to have mail from the kids, including pictures of them. He would like to make phone calls to the kids as well. He and Sandra discussed the issue of his visitation with the kids; Sandra decided not to bring the kids to visit Tom early in his incarceration, but to wait and see how they felt about the issue later on. Tom told Sandra that he wanted to remain an "active parent" to the highest degree possible while he was in prison, but that he was not sure how to do this. He decided to discuss this with his counselor.

Tom's mother is still living, and Tom decided to approach his mom about visiting him and exchanging phone calls and letters. He hoped this would help him understand his relationship with his own children. Tom told Sandra that he was not sure what to say and what not to say in his visits, letters, or phone calls. How much detail about his life in prison would be too much? Tom and Sandra discussed how their family lives might be different when Tom returned home if he made parole or served out his sentence.

# TIPS ON STAYING CLOSE TO FAMILY MEMBERS WHILE IN PRISON

To make the most of staying close to your family, consider these tips:

Be completely honest with the adults in your life before you are transferred to prison. Take responsibility for your crime, and let them know which educational opportunities and alcohol/drug programs — if needed — you believe are right for you. Ask them to come to visit with you as often as they can, and also ask if you can call them on the phone. Let them know that when you are released, you would like to come and see them or live with them.

If you have children who are old enough to understand the criminal justice and prison systems, here is an example of what you could say or write:

*"Daddy/Mommy has done something very wrong, and now I have to be punished for this by going to prison for a few years. Remember when you would do something wrong and be sent to your room as punishment? That is what is happening to me. But I want you to know that I am safe, I will always love you, and I'll always be your daddy/mommy. I would like for you to come and*

*visit me in prison, but you do not have to if you do not want to.*
*I would also like for us to write letters to each other, and I will*
*call you on the phone as much as I can. I hope you can send me*
*pictures of you and tell me all about what you are doing in school*
*and (hobbies such as ballet, or sports). If you have a problem, just*
*write to me and tell me all about it. I will help you figure out what*
*to do. I will not be home for Christmas or your birthday, but you*
*will get a special present from me that I bought with the money*
*I earned in prison and saved just for you. Even though I am not*
*there, I love you and I will be thinking about you all the time.*
*When I come home from prison, we will laugh and play just like*
*we used to. I promise I'll be a better daddy/mommy and that I will*
*never leave you again."*

In her book *Loving Through Bars*, Cynthia Martone wrote that more than 2.3 million children in the United States have a parent in prison. They, too, are prisoners in a jail without bars. They face the very difficult task of learning to live with a parent behind bars and learning to love that parent *through* bars. Regardless of the reason you are in prison, your child still loves and needs you to be as active in his or her life as possible. If you ignore your children while you are in jail, it can have a lasting negative effect on your child. A rejected or abandoned child never forgets this horrible feeling. You can and must maintain a relationship with your children while you are in prison through letters, visits, and phone calls.

Young children understand very little about prison and the criminal justice system. Suppose an inmate goes to "the hole" for disciplinary reasons. Imagine how horrified a child must feel, believing that his or her parent is literally shut up into a hole, which is actually a term for administrative segregation. It is up to you to make sure your young children understand the true picture of prison life. We can use Tom's story as an example of choices you will have to make about preparing your children for your incarceration.

## EXPLAINING TO YOUR CHILDREN WHERE YOU ARE

Over time, Tom noticed that his friend Jorge never visited with his two young children, although his wife did visit him. When Tom asked him about this, Jorge said that the children were told that Daddy was out of town working on a job and would not be back for a few years. Thinking of his own family, Tom asked around and found out that some inmates' children were told that Daddy was in a hospital or away from home going to college. One inmate said that his ex-wife told his children that he was dead.

Tom's crime and conviction was well-known in their community and had been in the newspapers. He did not want to lie to his children about where he was. He and his wife, Sandra, decided that the children would be told that Dad was in prison, and that both of them would explain fully to the children what prison was all about, that he was safe there, and that he would be coming back to the family. Sandra was still uncertain about the children going to visit Tom, but would encourage them to write letters to their father, and Tom would be able to talk with them on the phone as well. If this went well, Sandra told Tom that she would reconsider letting the children visit Tom if they chose to do so.

## *Visits from family members*

Making the most of phone calls, visits, and letters with your family can be tricky. Focus on positive experiences and conversation when communicating with your family, especially with your kids. For example, talk about what you are studying in your educational classes, friends you have made, how much you are enjoying your work assignment, and the fact that you no longer use drugs or alcohol. There is no need to reveal that last night there was a gang fight between two gangs. Information like this will not make your family sleep easily at night.

Visits with your children do matter. This will earn their respect, reduce the stress they are experiencing because of having an incarcerated mother or father, and will make you much less likely to commit another crime. When you are released, you can expect that resuming your role in your family will go much more smoothly. You can also expect to adjust better to life in your community. Even before you are released, visits and phone calls to your family will encourage you to follow prison rules so you will not lose these privileges. If this works in prison, it will also work once you are released.

Author Nell Bernstein makes the important point that during infancy and a child's first year, it is important for the child to be touched and held by his or her incarcerated mother or father. This increases the bond between them. Physical contact with the child also has a very positive impact on the parent. Without bodily contact during visits, it is hardly possible to develop a relationship with a young child. Bernstein compares "touch" visits with "window" visits where there is a glass barrier between an inmate's visitors and the inmate. Window visits are more common in county jails rather than prisons.

You will have to visit your children in a crowded visitors' room, but you can create your own private space with your children by focusing only on them and not what is going on in the rest of the room. For security reasons, you cannot have a private visitation room. If your older children have difficulty talking with you in a crowded room, you can encourage them to put all their thoughts, feelings, and problems in their letters instead. You might want to use your visits for merely touching, hugging, and interacting with your children in other physical manners. Braid or brush your daughter's hair, put your son on your lap and hug him when he tells you he made the Little League team, play cards or board games, have a gentle wrestling game with your son and let him win. There are many more ways you can physically interact with your children.

Unfortunately, there is a down side to keeping active in your children's lives. One problem is that a large number of prisons are located in rural areas. Bernstein wrote that more that 60 percent of prisons are more than 100 miles away from the inmate's home community, and federal prisons can be located anywhere in the United States. For many families, a spouse's job, the children's school, a lack of transportation, and the money involved in visiting the incarcerated parent can seriously diminish the number of times children get to see a parent who is in prison. One solution to this problem is to ask the judge who issues your sentence to send you to the prison that is closest to your family. Such requests are often granted, but your custody and security level may be too high for the minimum-security prison close to your family. In this case, and depending on your crime and the length of your sentence, you may be able to earn your way into a less secure prison closer to home by always following prison rules, never failing to practice good behavior, and staying out of trouble.

## *Phone calls*

Phone contact in prison is not as easy as just picking up the phone and dialing. If your behavior is poor, you may be denied this privilege. Inmates are not allowed to receive calls, and they can only make collect calls to their families. Collect calls are much more expensive than standard calls, and your family may not be able to afford them. When you want to make a call, you will be standing in line for a while, so be patient. Calls are usually limited to 15 minutes. Imagine cramming everything you want to say to your family and everything they want to say to you into this short length of time. This is nearly impossible if you have a spouse or partner and three young children. Again, writing letters to each other can come to the rescue. There is no limit on how much mail you can send or receive, and there are no restrictions on the length of any letters. It may not be as emotionally satisfying as visitation and phone calls, but letter writing has kept many families close when a parent is in prison. In addition, you can send money you earn in prison to your family to help pay for collect phone calls instead of using your money to buy snacks in the commissary. Remaining close to your family involves many influential choices and actions on your part; you have every reason to keep your family bond. You must think past yourself and your needs and think primarily about your spouse/partner and children's needs. When you can think of the best interests of others instead of yourself, you will have come a long way in your rehabilitation and readiness to re-enter society.

To conclude this chapter, let us check your understanding of the material you read here.

## Check Your Understanding No. 16

1. True or False: You should not tell your children that you are in prison so they will not worry about you.

2. True or False: You cannot be an active part of your child's life while you are in prison.

3. True or False: Ongoing contact with your family is the most important factor in whether you will reunite with them when you are released from prison.

4. True or False: Incarcerated parents and their very young children need to touch each other often to create a bond between them.

5. True or False: Writing letters is not helpful in keeping inmates involved in their children's lives.

# 8 What You and Your Family Will Go Through

In the criminal justice system, children are invisible. The system focuses on the crime, who committed that crime, convicting that person, and sending him or her to prison. In many ways, even the victim of the crime is less visible than the person who committed it. No one in the system takes the time to explain to children what happens when their parent is arrested, convicted, and sent to prison; not the police, the judge, or the DA. This unpleasant job is usually left to the social workers who work in shelters, group homes, or the foster care system. They do not know the child or the child's relationship with the incarcerated parent. An overworked social worker only has a case file. Again, the child is invisible. Many of these children come from single-parent homes, and when the adult goes to prison, the child is not only invisible, but also totally alone.

No doubt you are having a hard time adjusting to the fact that you will be in prison to serve your sentence, and that it is difficult to adjust to prison life if you are a "first-timer." It is important for you to understand that while you are having difficulty with being incarcerated, your children, parents, and spouse or partner are also going through extreme adjustment issues; it is not all about you. The victim of your crime is undergoing emotional turmoil as well, but for the purposes of this book, we need to focus on the secondary victims of your crime — your family members. Every inmate is someone's son, daughter, wife, husband, partner, mother, or father. In this chapter, we will examine how your family members will be affected by your incarceration and what you can do to make their lives easier and more meaningful while you are in prison.

## YOUR CHILDREN

All children want to know who their parents are. This explains why so many adopted children decide to find their birth parents. Children also want to know where their parents are. Many parents leave town often on business matters or in military service. Children of these parents want to know where Mommy or Daddy is and when he or she is coming back. Without this knowledge, children can feel neglected, rejected, or abandoned. Children of parents in prison may have poor self-esteem, low educational goals, behavior problems, or alcohol and other drug abuse issues. Or they may simply feel lonely, unfulfilled, and lost. It is often said that it is better to have a parent in prison than no parent at all.

When you went through the process of the criminal justice system, your children went through it with you. Yet, depending upon their age, they understood it far less than you did. You had an attorney to guide you and explain the process; your children did not. More often than not, children have many unanswered questions about the justice system, including incarceration. When children do not have these answers, they tend to imagine the worst.

In most cases, but not all, it is best to honestly answer your children's questions about incarceration and your involvement with the criminal justice system. Children who are age 7 or older are capable of understanding more than you may think. Speak in simple terms, and keep your tone positive. If you are angry or sad, your children are likely to feel the same. Plan what you are going to say in advance, and keep it brief because children have short attention spans. Imagine your 11-year-old son being made fun of at school because his daddy is a jailbird.

Give him the tools that he needs to hold his head up high: "Yeah, my dad's in jail, so what? He did something wrong and he is taking his punishment like a real man. I talk to him a lot and he says he will never break the law again when he comes home, and I believe him. He's my dad, and I'm proud of him no matter what." As you can see, it is important that you take responsibility for your actions and "man up" — or "be a woman" — and do the right thing. This gives your children something to be proud of instead of being ashamed of you. Children firmly believe in the proverb that the apple does not fall far from the tree; if you are "bad," then so are they. Let them know that you will serve your time with honor and dignity, and they can rely on you to be their parent both during your incarceration and when you return home.

A common question for both incarcerated parents and their children is whether a child of a criminal will grow up to be a criminal himself or herself. There is no easy or certain answer to this question because there are too many factors to be considered. In August 2004, President George W. Bush and the Office of Minority Health's resource center issued a press release that provided $45.6 million in grant money to provide positive mentors

— or role models — for the children of incarcerated parents. The press release stated, "The research had found that significant physical absence of a parent has profound effects upon child development. Children of incarcerated parents are seven times more likely to become involved in the juvenile and adult criminal justice system."

## *Your children's behavior*

This does not mean that your child is destined to grow up to break the law and become incarcerated just because you did. Committing crimes is a choice and not an inherited behavior. While you are incarcerated, unless you step up to the plate and be an active, involved part of your child's life, he or she will have no positive role models and is more likely to commit crimes. We can put this issue to rest by emphasizing a few extremely important points:

- If you and your spouse or partner have a history of criminal behavior and have no plans to change, your child will learn this behavior from you.

- If you admit your errors, take responsibility for your crime(s), correct your behavior, and accept your punishment with honor and dignity, your child will also learn this behavior from you.

- If you distance yourself from your child's life while you are incarcerated and are not an active parent, your child will feel confused and abandoned. He or she will develop a poor self-esteem and is more likely to commit crimes.

- If you stay very involved in your child's life in a loving and responsible way, your child will feel that love and acceptance and is not likely to commit crimes.

Your choices about how you live your life and how involved you are with your children is up to you. Keep in mind that every choice you make, good or bad, affects your children's future.

## Child welfare

If you are a single parent with a child, it is possible that your child may be placed in the state's custody and enter the foster care system while you are in prison. Although most single parents are women, it is not unusual for men to raise a child, especially if the mother is not involved in the child's life due to drug addiction, mental illness, or is incarcerated. Another important issue is the incarceration of pregnant women who will have their children at some point during their prison term.

It is important for you to realize that the image of the foster care system you see fictionalized on television is mostly inaccurate and unfair. Sure, there are a few bad apples among foster homes, just as there are with COs and other prison staff members. But the majority of foster homes are loving, caring, and work toward the eventual re-unification of children with their natural parents.

For your assurance, you should be aware of three important points: (1) The child welfare agency in your state will do everything possible to place your child/children with a relative who will properly care for them while you are in prison; (2) if this is not possible, the state will instead take custody of your child/children and place them into foster care while you are in prison;

and (3) depending on your crime and the length of your sentence, your parental rights may be permanently terminated and your child/children placed in a foster home pending adoption. This means that you have no legal right to see, write to, call, or visit with your child/children. Bernstein wrote that it is important to stay in contact with the child in order to eventually regain parental rights and to successfully rehabilitate. However, it is difficult for prisoners because they face tremendous obstacles to maintain relationships with children in foster care.

## Social workers

If you wish to reunite with your child/children after you are released from prison, you will be working with social workers from your state's child welfare agency. Many social workers who work for the state are overloaded with a huge amount of cases; they receive low pay, and the burnout level among them is high. However, it is important for you to know that the vast majority of social workers truly do care about you and your child or children, and they will gladly work with you to set up a plan to reunite you with your little ones after you are released from prison. Perhaps this re-unification will help you make sure you obey all prison rules and stay out of trouble, and perhaps it will inspire you to attend parenting classes, substance abuse treatment, and educational classes to demonstrate that you have a strong desire to be a parent to your child or children.

If you have children who are capable of understanding the way the criminal justice system and the foster care system works, it is best if you can explain this to them through a visit, letter, or phone call. For example:

*"Mommy/Daddy did something wrong, and now I have to be punished for this by going to prison. Do not worry: We will all be safe, and we will see each other soon. You will be in a foster home with adults who love you and will take care of your needs. They will do for you what I cannot do for now. When I have completed my punishment and am out of prison, we will have the help of social workers to make sure we all come together as a family again. I love you, and I will always be thinking of you."*

## Sex offenders and their children

This section would not be complete without a brief discussion about sex offenders and their children. If you are incarcerated for the sexual assault of a minor child and you have children of your own, it is reasonably certain that your parental rights regarding your own children will be terminated by a court of law. The most up-to-date social research on child molestation indicates that people who sexually abuse minor children begin by molesting their own children in their own homes. They then "graduate" into molesting children outside the home. If this situation applies to you, it is best if you serve your sentence and attend all the sexual offender rehabilitation programs the prison offers, and then wait until your children are adults before you contact them. It is possible that they will not want to talk with you or see you. Understand that you caused this rift between yourself and your children, and that you can only hope to mend this rift.

It is time to check your understanding of the material presented so far in this chapter.

## Check Your Understanding No. 17

1. True or False:    Your children are undergoing as much stress as you are while you are in prison.

2. True or False:    If your parental rights are terminated, your children are no longer interested in finding you.

3. True or False:    Because you have committed crimes, your children are genetically destined to also commit crimes and be incarcerated.

4. True or False:    All foster care homes are uncaring and brutal toward the children placed with them.

5. True or False:    Inmates who have committed sexual assaults against minors could have their parental rights terminated.

# YOUR SPOUSE OR PARTNER

If you had a close, loving relationship with your spouse or partner, he or she will find it difficult to carry on with the daily routine of living, especially if your partner became an unwilling single parent when you went to prison. The single, most important thing you can do in this situation is to continually tell your partner that you know he or she is having a hard time and that you are truly sorry to have caused such distress. Acknowledge that life without your physical, emotional, and financial support may be difficult — it will go a long way to ease your partner's anger and frustration about your absence. Reassure him or her that you will be the "model prisoner" so you can make parole as soon as possible and that you will take advantage of all the opportunities in prison that will help you never have to go back again.

Here are some pointers to consider if you truly want your marriage or relationship to last while you are in prison:

- Keep in contact through frequent letters, phone calls, and visits.

- Ask about your prison's policy on conjugal visits; if they are allowed, use them. Physical intimacy is very helpful if you and your partner want to keep your relationship intact.

- Through your prison work program, send your partner as much money as you possibly can. Anything is better than nothing, and it lets your partner know that you still feel responsible for his or her welfare. If there is a financial crisis at home, ask your counselor or case manager for a list of agencies that can help, such as churches, the Salvation Army, and other private charities that help the families of incarcerated family members.

- When your partner visits you, do not use the time merely to ask him or her to bring you things, make phone calls to others for you, put money into your prison account, or other things that benefit you. Do not be a "bottomless pit" of demands upon your partner; he or she will soon feel used by you rather than loved and cherished by you.

- Do not subject your partner to endless questions about what he or she is doing and if he or she is seeing someone else, and do not try to be overly controlling of his or her actions. This type of jealously will only drive your partner away from you. Make your partner feel wanted, not threatened.

- Ask reasonable and non-demanding questions about your partner's life. Show a sincere interest in him or her. Ask about your partner's parents or other relatives. Ask about anything that is important in your partner's life, such as school or work.

Keep in mind this general rule: Whenever you have any kind of contact with your spouse or partner, focus on his or her needs and life, not yours. If you fail to do this, it becomes more likely that he or she will discover that life can continue just fine without you and that your presence is not as desirable as originally thought when you first went to prison. The quickest way to be "written off" by your partner is to be selfish, jealous, and demanding.

## YOUR PARENTS

If this is your first time in prison, you may have parents who are extremely worried about how you will cope with prison life and what life will hold for you in the future as an ex-convict. Consider these pointers:

- Before you are transferred to prison, have a long talk with your parents in person or on the phone. If this is not possible, write a letter. Tell them that you have read this book and that you feel prepared to face whatever prison life holds for you.

- Accept responsibility for the offense that you committed and responsibility for your rehabilitation while you are in prison. This will reassure them that you know what you did was wrong and that you will never do it again.

- Many parents believe that it is their fault that you committed a crime because they were bad parents; they did not teach you right from wrong. While it is true that some prison inmates did not have parents who were interested in teaching them correct morals or values, many inmates had parents who truly did their very best to raise their children to live within the law. If this is your case, tell your parents that it is not their fault that you are in prison. This goes along with accepting responsibility for your actions and not blaming anyone else.

- On the other hand, perhaps you did not have a good upbringing from your parents. There may have been crime, drugs, alcohol, or domestic violence in your home when you were young. In this case, your parents may want to apologize for not teaching you right from wrong. Accept their apology. You may still have negative feelings about a parent and how you were treated when you were young, but you can still acknowledge their apology. This is not the same as forgiving someone. It is simply having the courage to be kind.

- Your parents will be worried about your safety in prison. Reassure them that you know how to keep yourself safe and what to do if you feel you are in danger from another inmate. Let them know that you are not going to join a prison gang, disobey the COs, or break prison rules. As with your children, you need not tell your parents about distressing or even violent events in prison in which you were not involved.

It is time to check your understanding of this material before we end this chapter.

## Check Your Understanding No. 18

1. True or False:   Your spouse or partner needs your emotional support while you are in prison.

2. True or False:   Jealous behavior on your part will show your partner how much you still love him or her.

3. True or False:   It is your partner's responsibility to meet all your needs while you are in prison.

4. True or False:   It is always your parents' fault that you are in prison because they failed to raise you correctly.

5. True or False:   Because of Hollywood stereotypes, your parents will fear for your safety while you are in prison.

# CHAPTER 9

# Women in Prison

If you are a woman going to prison for the first time, this chapter is for you and your loved ones. You will find answers to many of the most common questions and issues facing incarcerated women. Hopefully, pointed and honest information about what you can expect and what you are experiencing will banish your fears about what to expect in prison. Knowing the truth always reduces stress and provides hope for the future.

Most of the information about prison in this book pertains to both men and women inmates. For example, just like the men reading this book, you need to know facts about the assessment and classification system; the evaluation you will experience when you first come to prison; information about your medical care; how to arrange for family visits; your legal status and rights while you are serving your time; and the general rules of most state prisons. Like men, you will receive an inmate's handbook that contains these rules as well as other valuable information about the prison. Still, women inmates have unique issues and needs that must be addressed. In this chapter, we will use an additional case study about a woman named Glory to provide appropriate examples for you.

## GLORY'S STORY

Glory is a 27-year-old woman who was transferred to the state prison after being convicted of the possession of narcotics and receiving stolen property. She was sentenced to seven years in prison and can apply for parole after serving three years. Glory's boyfriend is a known drug trafficker and has been sentenced to prison for five counts of first-degree burglary. She is five months pregnant by her boyfriend; she became pregnant while on a weekend pass from the county jail. Her boyfriend was physically and emotionally abusive to Glory, resulting in her low self-esteem and lack of confidence.

Glory has a 6-year-old son named James who has lived with Glory's mother since he was born due to Glory's history of drug abuse, unemployment, and helping her boyfriend sell the property that he steals during home burglaries. James does not know his real father, a drug addict who left Glory when she told him she was pregnant with James. Glory dropped out of high school and has no technical skills, although she has above-average intelligence. Her father, a now-deceased alcoholic, used to beat her with a belt if she did not do well in school. She has never participated in any sort of drug abuse treatment program. Since Glory has no prior convictions and no history of disruptive behavior prior to sentencing, the classification team placed Glory in administrative segregation for 60 days to complete her prison orientation; she will then be placed in general population in the women's unit.

# WOMEN'S ISSUES IN PRISON

From Glory's example, we can see many common issues facing women in prison:

- History of alcohol and drug abuse

- History of being sexually and/or physically abused as a child

- Current/recent history of domestic violence

- Lack of self-esteem and confidence

- Lack of education and job skills

- History of property crimes related to domestic violence and drug abuse

- Current pregnancy

- Other school-age children with "absent" fathers

- Being the child of a drug addict or alcoholic

In her book *War on the Family: Mothers in Prison and the Families They Leave Behind*, Renny Golden describes female drug and alcohol addicts as "collateral damage in the war on drugs," meaning that most women who become addicted have a boyfriend or husband who is involved in drug trafficking. Since the U.S. government began to crack down on this 20 years ago, the incarceration rate rose almost 30 percent among men and women for drug-related crimes. About 70 percent of all female inmates are mothers of small children. Golden believes that when women go to prison, all family bonds are broken and the children are left without the only biological parent they have.

We often wonder whether a female inmate would have committed crimes without the presence of male drug users and traffickers in their lives. At any rate, you should keep in mind that when you go to prison and are separated from your children, it is extremely important that you maintain your family bond with them through visits, mail, and phone calls. Also, you should take every opportunity to participate in drug and alcohol abuse programs to help you get clean and stay clean without a return trip to prison. Golden wrote that when an incarcerated mother receives successful treatment in a rehabilitation program, completes a GED or high school education program, obtains job-training skills, and maintains contact with her children, the end of a family separation is very promising after she serves her sentence or is paroled.

As long as your self-esteem and confidence in yourself is low, it is unlikely that you will be able to stay clean and sober and avoid domestic abuse when you are released from prison. We can use Glory's story to illustrate this point.

## GROUPS CAN HELP

When Glory was transferred to gen pop, she found that her cellie, Deborah, was very active in the prison's substance rehabilitation program. She also attended group therapy three times a week to overcome negative feelings about herself and her future. Glory decided to attend these programs too because Deborah said they were very helpful to her. Glory was surprised to find that the majority of women in both programs were also mothers, had suffered abuse as a child and with their husbands or boyfriends, and had little education.

"I latched onto any man I could find," Deborah told Glory during group therapy. "The only thing that made me feel good about myself was when a man wanted me. I had no job and no education to get one. My men got money by stealing from houses and stores and selling drugs. When

I turned tricks (had sex for money) for drug money, he beat the hell out of me. I was shooting heroin when I was pregnant with Daren, my 9-year-old. The state took him from me when he was only 2, and I don't even know where he is. He wouldn't even know me now."

Glory told the group that her son, James, was teased and bullied by other children because his mother was a jailbird. "He's always in trouble for beating up kids who make fun of him," Glory said. "I know he blames me for all this. I don't know if he even wants to visit me in jail anymore."

Reading Glory's and Deborah's story, it is easy to see that separation from your children during your incarceration is extremely painful for both you and your kids. In her book *All Alone in the World*, Nell Bernstein wrote that while it is difficult for children to see their mothers in prison, family visits build a "tent of intimacy that shelters and unites them." Staying close to your kids will make your time in prison both easier to bear and will give you and your child hope for the future.

## PREGNANT IN PRISON

It is not uncommon for women to come to prison while they are pregnant and give birth in custody of the prison. Prison physicians are very familiar with pregnancy issues, so you will receive good pre-natal care. If you experience a problem that is beyond the skill of your physician, he or she will send you to a local civilian specialist. In most prisons, women have their babies in a community hospital in case they experience a labor or delivery problem. It may help you to know that even though you are incarcerated, prison staff members will take your pregnancy and delivery seriously. You should take care of your own health while you are pregnant; eat regular healthy meals, get plenty of fresh air and exercise during recreation periods in the prison yard, and take all medications — including pre-natal vitamins — prescribed by your doctor.

If your pregnancy is complicated because you suffer from HIV, hepatitis, or tuberculosis, your prison physician will need to see you more often and develop a special medical plan for you and your unborn child. Author Silja Talvi states that prison inmates are eight to nine times more likely to be suffering from HIV or hepatitis; African American women inmates are the group more likely to have these life-threatening illnesses. Since you will be tested for pregnancy and for many dangerous diseases when you are first admitted to prison, you will receive up-to-date medical care during your pregnancy.

Let us check your understanding of the material presented so far in this chapter.

## Check Your Understanding No. 19

1. True or False:     More women are convicted of drug-related offenses than any other crime.

2. True or False:     It is not possible for you to maintain a bond with your children during your incarceration.

3. True or False:     You can help rehabilitate yourself by participating in therapy and educational programs.

4. True or False:     In most cases, women give birth in the prison hospital.

5. True or False:   Many female inmates were abused during their childhoods.

# CHILD CUSTODY

If women have children, or give birth while they are inmates, one of the most common issues they face is whether they will maintain custody of their children. It is important that you understand that going to prison does not automatically make you an unfit mother; in most cases, the state will not take custody of your children simply because you are an inmate. In fact, children of incarcerated mothers are only taken into the state's custody when there are no relatives who are willing and capable of caring for these children. We can use Glory's example to illustrate this point.

## WHO GETS CUSTODY?

During a group therapy session, Mae, a new inmate, said that she was very worried about her children. "They're just kids, and they're worried about what will happen to them now. Ceely is 12 and Nathan is 10. Their father told the social worker that because of his mental health problem, he can't take care of them. He has no job and lives on a little disability and veterans' benefits, not enough to pay for what they need. The social worker told me that they will take Ceely and Nathan into state custody or foster care only if nobody else in my family can take them. The child welfare people are checking out my Mom because she said she would take them."

During the next group session, Mae was smiling. "My Mom gets to keep the kids," she said. "The state will send some money to Mom to buy food and clothes for them, and she will bring them to visit me every week. I am really going to work hard to make parole so we can all put this behind us."

## *The foster care system*

Bernstein wrote that 12 percent of the children who have parents in prison were placed in foster care. The placement of your children into foster care usually happens if you have no fit and proper relatives who can care for them. State-employed child welfare social workers will visit with both you and your children to help determine the best custodial placement; great efforts are made to keep children with relatives who know and love them rather than with kind, but unknown, foster parents. The following points will be considered when determining if your relatives can provide care for your kids while you are in prison:

- **The relationship of the family member to your children.** Grandparents, aunts, uncles, and adult siblings are preferred placements, especially if your kids know them well and like them. Chances are, your kids would rather be with a family member who will help keep your family bonds strong than with a stranger who does not know your family's history.

- **The physical ability of the family member to care for your children.** Relatives who are elderly and/or disabled or handicapped in some way may not be able to cope with taking care of your kids, especially if a child has special physical, emotional, or educational needs. For example, an elderly grandmother may not be physically capable of caring for your very young child, but your aunt or older sister could be capable.

- **How well the family member is able to support your children financially.** If your kids are placed with a relative, he or she will receive money from the state to help pay for their basic needs. These funds are used for buying food and clothing, and also for making sure your kids have a good home to live in. However, in today's economy, this money does not cover items that are not absolutely necessary for your child. For example, your child may want to play sports in school or listen to popular music with friends. Athletic equipment and uniforms are expensive, as are stereos and music CDs. These luxury items may improve your child's quality of life, but they can be done without. It is important that you earn the privilege to work while you are in prison to help your relatives pay for the special things that make childhood more fulfilling.

- **The wishes of the child, and your wishes for the child's placement.** State social workers will certainly consider where you would like for your child to live, and they will take the child's wishes into account as well. However, your child's custody and placement is ultimately decided by what is in the best interest of the child. For example, your child may wish to live with his or her aunt; if she already has four young children of her own living in a cramped apartment, however, the social workers may look for another relative who can better provide a home for your child.

We can use Glory's case to illustrate some of these points.

## FOSTER AND FAMILY CARE

Before their parenting group session, Deborah could tell that Glory was upset about something. During group therapy, Glory said that her son James may not be able to continue living with her mother. "My mom is 78 years old and has to use a walker to get around since she broke her hip last fall," Glory said. "She loves James, but the social worker thinks that she might not be able to keep up with a young boy. My mom raised James because I was doing dope and turning tricks for drug money with my man."

Deborah said, "Is James going to have to go into foster care?"

Glory said she did not know. "My aunt lives in Boston, a long way from here. She wouldn't be able to bring James to see me, but my mom would."

Another inmate, Jessie, said, "My two kids are in foster care with the state, and they're both doing real well. The foster parents are licensed by the state, so they have to provide good care for my kids; a social worker comes to see them at least twice a month. The foster mom brings them to see me every week, and I write to them and call them as often as I can. When I get out, we'll still be as close as ever."

Glory shed a few tears and said, "What about my baby? If my mom can't keep taking care of James, she sure isn't going to be able to care for the baby. I'm afraid that if the state takes custody of my kids and puts them in foster care, I will never be able to see them. When I get out, the baby won't know me."

An inmate named Kathleen said, "I had my daughter while I was in prison. I know I messed up, but all I want is to be there for my kid. The social worker put her in a foster home when I got out of the hospital and couldn't keep her in prison. But she picked the baby up and brought her to me every week, and now it looks like my brother and his wife are going to be able to keep her until I get out."

The following week, Glory came to the group session smiling widely. "The state social worker talked to all of us, and James can stay with my mom, on the condition that he behaves well at home and school. The social worker warned him that if he acted up, he would have to go to a foster family or a group home."

"What about the baby?" Deborah asked.

Still smiling, Glory said, "My mom will take the baby, too. The social worker will get a nurse to come and see the baby every other day and help mom care for her." The group leader asked if all this good news would motivate Glory to make a favorable impression on the parole board.

"Oh, yes," said Glory. "I'm going to get my GED and then some technical training in computer word processing. I will keep coming to group, parenting classes, and substance abuse treatment. All I want is my family — I'm never coming back to prison."

## CHANGES IN WOMEN'S PRISONS

In the past 20 years, there have been many changes in women's prisons. Women are safer from sexual assault, prisons offer many more educational and therapeutic opportunities than in the past, and a major emphasis has been placed on maintaining family bonds. In her book, Renny Golden made the case that in the near future, women's prisons must be redesigned to include units for inmates who are nursing newborns; state-sponsored and volunteer programs that provide transportation to children and other family members who wish to visit an incarcerated loved one; and increased vocational job training skills training for women on parole.

All women — not just mothers — in prison are experiencing the benefits of major changes in the care and custody of female inmates. If you are not a mother or a wife, you still do not have to feel alone in prison. It may be a scary thing at first, but as you get used to the rules, the limits upon your personal freedom, and the strangers all around you, keep in mind that your life in prison will be what you make of it.

Some prisons are still dark and dangerous places. Our country is struggling with not only recognizing the changes that must be made, but also making sure that economic policies do not place a lower value on inmates simply because they are "throw-away" people. Today, you have the opportunity to not just read history, but to also make history.

Instead of only attending educational and therapeutic programs in your institution, speak up if you see the need for additional programs. In addition to prison staff members, your community most likely has volunteers who are waiting for opportunities to help you succeed in prison, make parole, and never again be imprisoned. If you are talented in a particular skill, teach other women who want to learn. For example, if you have a talent for making quilts, you and other women can turn this skill into a well-paying job opportunity in the community. If you are an excellent cook, teach others how they can use these skills in the kitchens of local restaurants. If you are an expert on cleaning your unit quickly and thoroughly, this too is a skill you and others can use to make money on the outside.

Everything you do well is a potential "money-maker" when you are released. Take pride in your skills, whatever they may be. Teach your skills to other women, and use those skills to help yourself and others avoid parole violations that result in a return to prison. You will find that serving your time will go much faster if you maintain your dignity, keep your mind and hands busy, and have your eyes on the prize. By setting goals for yourself and always making strides to achieve those goals, you need not ever lose your freedom again.

## Check Your Understanding No. 20

1. True or False: If you go to prison, you will automatically lose custody of your children.

2. True or False: In most cases, it is better for your children to be placed with a relative while you are incarcerated.

3. True or False: Your wishes will be taken into consideration regarding the care and custody of your children.

4. True or False: Women are safer from sexual assaults in prison than in the past.

5. True or False: Every skill you have can be taught to other inmates.

# CHAPTER 10

# How to Keep Your Mind Right While You Are in Prison

You will discover in prison that unless you maintain your sense of self-worth and conduct yourself with dignity, it is likely that you will lose all sense of who you are and what your place is in the world. For now, you are an inmate. What you do in prison and whether you learn to think of yourself in a positive manner will actually determine your future. You have the option of changing your thinking and your behavior so you can leave prison as a better person than when you went inside, or you can spend your time becoming a "prison thug." If this is how you want to live your life, do not be surprised when you end up right back in jail.

We can use Tom's case as an example of how to keep your dignity while you are incarcerated.

## CHANGING THE WAY YOU FEEL ABOUT YOURSELF

One day in Tom's group therapy addiction treatment, another inmate, Norris, told the group that he felt like his addiction to heroin took away his sense of self-worth. "I would do anything for a fix," Norris told the group. "It did not matter how low I had to stoop. When I was jonesing (craving drugs), nothin' mattered except getting a fix. I stopped being a man the day I became a junkie."

Tom said, "I think I understand how you feel. When I was not drinking, I was thinking about drinking and not caring about anything else except my next drink." The group's therapist, Jane, said, "Norris, you have been in prison now for three years. Do you think you have changed how you feel about yourself since you have been an inmate?"

Norris replied, "Yeah, I have changed. And not just because I can't shoot up in prison, either. The drug not only ate away at my body, it ate away at my heart and soul too. Then I came to prison, and I sank even lower. That first year was tough because I had given up on myself. I spent more days in segregation than anyone I know. Now that I'm clean, I see myself as a man again, even though I'm in prison to pay for my crimes. I want to get out of here and live a decent life, not like a rat in a sewer."

Jane said, "The way I see it, you guys can come into prison with no sense of dignity, or you can come in with your dignity and lose it while you are in here. Either way, how you feel about yourself is going to determine what your behavior in and out of prison will be in the future."

# PRISONIZATION

A term you must become familiar with is "prisonization." When you first become an inmate, you will learn how to behave with other inmates, the values they have, their roles in the prison society, and their special language. By the time you become used to prison, you will have become a "con." Going through this process is necessary to help you adjust to being an inmate.

On the other hand, it is extremely important that you not build your sole identity and your dignity around being a con. Many prisoners become institutionalized, meaning that they become so used to their lives being rigidly structured that they cannot re-adjust to the freedoms found in society when they are released. These inmates will probably commit another crime once they get out of prison because they have become used to the prison way of life and are not disturbed by it; thus, the threat of being arrested is no longer a deterrent for them. With this in mind, the best thing you can do to preserve your dignity — and at the same time stay safe in prison — is to never see incarceration as an option in your future.

## HOW TO STAY POSITIVE

The following are some important things to remember about keeping your mind right in prison:

### *Humor*

Find the humor in any situation you can. No matter how dire your circumstances may be, you will cope with prison life better if you maintain your sense of humor. Rather than becoming bitter and depressed, when you see or hear something that deserves a good laugh, do so. You can also use humor to lighten the fears and problems of your family as well. We can use Tom's case as an example of this.

## STAYING POSITIVE

After visiting with his wife one afternoon, Tom came back to his cell and spoke to Randy about another inmate named Boxer. "I don't get it," Tom said to Randy. "Every time I see Boxer and his wife in the visiting room, they're always laughing and joking. What's so funny about being stuck in prison?"

That evening in the chow hall, Tom and Randy asked Boxer why he and his wife seemed to laugh a lot during visitation. "Man, I don't want to bum her out," said Boxer. "How's that gonna help anything? She's got a hard enough time taking care of the house and the kids until my parole."

"Well, what was so funny today?" Tom asked.

Boxer began to chuckle. "Aw, I just told her about how Simon is gonna sue the Department of Corrections for making him miss more than 100 meals. He said that he didn't get a wheelchair and couldn't go to chow. He told his lawyer that the DOC was trying to kill him."

"Wait a minute," said Randy. "Isn't Simon that really fat dude who always cries about being too fat to walk?"

"Yep," said Boxer. "Doesn't look to me like he's missed too many meals. Dude's just crazy, always tryin' to sue somebody. My wife said she'd bring him some cheesecake so he wouldn't starve to death." Shaking their heads, Tom, Randy, and Boxer laughed as they left the chow hall.

## *Using time wisely*

Put your time in prison to good use. You will find it much easier to get through your time in prison if you have something meaningful to do. We have already discussed educational services, hobbies, working to earn money, and going to therapy. There are even more opportunities for you to use your time in ways that will help you keep your mind straight. For example, in 2001, a story ran in a Florida newspaper about the involvement of state prison inmates in the guide dog training program. These programs are offered at many prisons. To take part, you will need to be on a low security and custody level with a record of good behavior. This is a job that must be taken seriously.

Inmates who raise puppies who will become guide dogs for the blind need to understand that their work will make a big difference in the life of a handicapped person. They are responsible for every aspect of a puppy's life, such as feeding, basic socialization skills, teaching the puppy to have good manners around people and other dogs, walking the puppy on a collar and leash, and cleaning kennels. Puppies usually stay with the inmates inside the prison from age 10 weeks to 15 months before they proceed to advanced training as guide dogs. In addition to being an excellent use of their time, this program provided the inmates with some companionship for a period of time, and it also helped many inmates earn their certification as veterinary technicians later — a valuable skill to have after parole.

## *Spirituality and religion*

You are not required to follow a religion or even be spiritual in any way; naturally, this is your personal preference. However, if you are a spiritual or religious person, it is important that you maintain your spirituality in prison. If you have been curious about a certain religion, this might be a good time for you to learn more about it, or to become more serious about your religion if you wish. Spirituality can be a great comfort to many inmates. You will find plenty of opportunities to practice your religion in prison to a reasonable degree. You can have access to the Holy Bible, the Qu'ran, the Book of Mormon, and other religious texts. You can also attend church services in prison if your behavior is good. You can put ministers or pastors on your visitors' list and also receive mail from them.

## Making friends with those on the outside

If you find yourself feeling lonely in prison, as if your friends and family have forgotten you, do whatever you can to maintain some sort of contact with the outside world. On the Internet, you will find many Web sites that publish inmates' stories and poems, sell paintings and other art works made by inmates, and provide "pen pal" correspondents who are willing to exchange letters with you. Keep in mind that you are not allowed to distribute pornography in any form, written or artistic. You are also not allowed to exchange letters of a sexual nature with a pen pal. Most importantly, never correspond in any way with a person younger than 18 years old. Be sure to check the prison's rules about these issues.

## Keep a clean spirit and mind

Stay "clean" in your body, mind, and spirit. Do not allow yourself to become involved in illegal practices in prison; keep your personal hygiene at top level; and do not dwell on anger, bitterness, or fear. Keep your eyes on the prize: your parole, your freedom, and your chance to start over again with a new way of life. You never again want to be in the custody of others. Surround yourself with other "clean-minded" inmates who have life goals and viewpoints similar to yours. Stay clear of violence, sex, drugs, and contraband. Clean living means showing the parole board that you are capable of being a member of society who will follow the rules. Unfortunately, during your prison sentence, you will see many inmates who are heavily involved in gangs, smuggling contraband, sexual assaults, and other types of criminal behavior. They dress, talk, and have tattoos that clearly indicate their outlaw status. Do not trust them, do not be intimidated by them, and do not fall into their destructive way of life.

## Stay away from crime while in prison

Some inmates love to talk about how mean and tough they are. Many times this is only talk meant to intimidate other inmates and staff. But sometimes, the talk is real. Specifically, you may hear talk about inmates staging a riot to protest living conditions or denial of privileges, or to create a diversion so they can harm rival gang inmates. In a prison riot, everyone loses. The Correctional Peace Officers Foundation's magazine, *CPO Family*, pays tribute to COs killed in the line of duty, many times during a breakout of prison violence. The taxpayers who provide funds for your custodial care must pay for damages to prisons where riots occur. Inmates who participate in and/or incite riots are prosecuted for these crimes and given additional prison time. No matter what you want, no matter what you believe you deserve, and no matter how angry you are, you will not achieve your goal by participating in prison violence. Stay away from all discussions of starting a riot, and remember the modern proverb: "When you see crazy coming your way, cross the street."

## Believe in yourself

Keep faith in yourself. There is no doubt that you will have some difficult days in prison. It is not an easy place to live. You will make some mistakes, and you will have some unpleasant interactions with other inmates and staff members. Just remember that you live in tight quarters with several thousand other inmates. Some of them are prone to violence. You must interact with COs who are often tired and always overworked and underpaid. You will not always get what you want in prison, but in the course of your journey, you just may discover what you really need.

Never lose sight of the fact that you have a release date, whether you make parole or you serve out your sentence. This is not forever. You will one day reclaim your freedom. As long as you keep this faith, you will find it easier to obey the rules, obtain your educational or vocational goals, and not let yourself become comfortable being a "con." Do not doubt that despite your hardships in prison life, you can change your life and never again look at the world through metal bars.

It is time to check your understanding of the material presented in this chapter.

## Check Your Understanding No. 21

1. True or False:   When you surrender your freedom, you also surrender your dignity.

2. True or False:   "Prisonization" means becoming accustomed to the way of life in prison.

3. True or False:   Putting your time in prison to good use will help you to keep your mind right.

4. True or False:   You are not allowed to attend church services or study holy books in prison.

5. True or False:   If you start or participate in a prison riot, you cannot be charged with any crime because you are already incarcerated.

# Conclusion

This book has covered a variety of subjects, many of which may frighten you but may also help you stay safe in prison. There is no doubt prison is a scary place. Still, it can be a place where you receive work and educational opportunities that you have never been offered before you were sentenced to prison. Learning a job skill and increasing your educational level will be crucial when you are released from prison and are seeking a job. If you want to remain "free," then you must be prepared to work hard and study hard during your time in prison, always keeping in mind your goal to never return.

During your coming incarceration, you will have an abundance of time — as well as assistance from staff members and other inmates — to help you discover who you really are. Yes, you are now a criminal. But this word does not totally define your true self. You may be a loving partner and parent; you may have a curious mind that will allow you to learn new educational and technical skills; you may have a strong work ethic; and you may be a true American who believes in choosing the right behavior over wrong behavior simply because it is, morally and ethically, the correct thing to do. If you know who you are and are true to yourself, it will be impossible for you to lie, steal, abuse alcohol and other drugs, or harm others. You can rejoin society and be of no risk to others.

I cannot emphasize strongly enough how important it is for you to maintain a family relationship while you are in prison. In my experience as a correctional officer, I quickly learned that the "cons" who had no family or friends on the outside with whom they could exchange letters, phone calls, and visits gradually retreated completely into the "con" ways of thinking and acting. Find someone to reach out to. Being locked inside a prison can result in an inmate's searching for the only human contact possible: other cons, gangs, and violence.

I hope that this book has helped you by answering many of your — and your family's — questions and fears about what prison life is like. It is not an easy life, nor should it be. After all, you did commit the crime that landed you in prison. But being incarcerated and then making parole can reverse the course of your life — if you let it. Your future is in your hands.

As a final parting thought, I would like to leave you with this Turkish phrase: *Getchmis olsun*, or, "May it pass quickly."

# Appendix A: Criminal Law and Procedure Terms

## CRIMINAL LAW TERMS

**Accessory** — A person who helps another person *before or after* he or she commits a crime; also called "an accessory after the fact" or "an accessory before the fact."

**Accomplice** — A person who helped another person or persons commit a crime.

**Affirmative defense** — A defense where the defendant has the burden of proof; often used in insanity defenses, entrapment, or coercion.

**Aforethought** — Planned in advance.

**Aggravated** — A crime that involves the use or brandishing (showing) of a weapon.

**Appeal** — A convicted person's request that a higher court, called an appellate court, review the trial proceedings of the lower court to take note of a specific error by the judge in matters of law and criminal procedure; a higher court can affirm (agree with) the lower court, reverse the verdict and enter a new verdict, or remand (send back) the case for retrial in the lower court.

**Appellant** — A person who appeals a lower court's decision to a higher court.

**Arson** — Intentionally burning a structure.

**Arrest** — The act by law enforcement officers of taking a suspect in a crime into physical custody; an arrest occurs when the suspect is no longer free to leave police custody.

**Assault** — An attempt to commit a battery or intentionally putting another person in fear of harm.

**Balloon swallowers** — Drug smugglers who fill balloons or condoms with drugs, which they ingest into their stomachs and intestines.

**Bail** — Money or property deposited to the court to secure the release of a defendant from jail pending trial; the U.S. Constitution guarantees the right of "reasonable" bail depending on the defendant's ability to pay, the seriousness of the charge, and the possibility that the defendant may be a flight risk. The entire bail amount is forfeited if the defendant does not appear in court, and a bench warrant is issued for his or her arrest *without* bail.

**Bail bondsman** — A person whose business is to provide bail for defendants in custody awaiting trial; the bondsman's fee is usually 10 percent of the amount of the bail posted.

**Ballistics** — The analysis of firearms, ammunition, bombs, and explosives; most often seen as evidence determining whether a particular bullet came from a particular firearm by examining the markings on the bullet after it has been fired.

**Battery** — Offensive or harmful bodily contact with another person; this usually goes together with an assault.

**Bench warrant** — An arrest warrant issued directly by the judge; usually seen with defendants who fail to appear for trial after posting bail.

**Booking** — A law enforcement process that enters a suspect formally into custody after arrest, the place the suspect was arrested, the time of arrest, the reason for arrest, and the name of the arresting officer.

**Bounty hunter** — More correctly called a fugitive recovery agent. These are people hired by a bail bondsman to find and capture defendants for whom they have posted bail but did not appear for trial.

**Breaking** — In a burglary, an illegal entry into another person's building.

**Burden of proof** — The legal duty to prove a point that is in dispute; also called the responsibility to produce evidence that convinces a judge or jury of a defendant's guilt.

**Burglary** — Breaking and entering a building with the intent of committing a crime inside the building, such as stealing or sexual assault.

**Capital felony** — A felony that is punishable by death or life in prison without parole.

**Career criminal** — A person with many arrests and convictions for illegal acts.

**Chain of custody** — The *unbroken* line of police authorities who collect and process evidence at a crime scene. Frequently, this is an appeal issue if the chain is questionable and the evidence could have been tampered with.

**Child abuse** — The crime of physically, sexually, or emotionally harming a child; can be intentional or negligent.

**Circumstantial evidence** — Evidence that is not observed directly but can be inferred as pointing to a defendant's guilt; frequently an appeal issue since it can be unreliable.

**Civil death** — In some jurisdictions, inmates are not allowed to vote, hold public office, marry, or enter into contracts. In other jurisdictions, inmates can marry and even have children through "conjugal visits," where they are given permission to have sex with a legal spouse in the prison.

**Clemency** — A decision by the government in which the severity of the punishment of an inmate or group of inmates is reduced, stopped, or prosecution is not allowed.

**Club drug** — Substances often found in nightclubs; includes MDMA (Ecstasy), Ketamine, GHB, Rohypnol, and methamphetamine. All are illegal to possess or manufacture.

**Conspiracy** — An agreement between two or more people to commit a crime.

**Contempt of court** — The crime of intentionally disobeying a court order; usually seen in failure to appear in court, violation of protective orders, and unruly behavior in court.

**Conversion** — Illegal use of another person's property without the owner's consent.

*Corpus delicti* — Latin term meaning "the body of the crime." It is the prosecutor's duty to present facts that show that a crime has been committed.

**Credit card fraud** — The crime of using or attempting to use another person's credit card to make purchases without the intent of paying for them.

**Criminal attempt** — Intending to commit a crime and taking steps to commit it but being interrupted before the completion of the crime.

**Culpability** — Being responsible in some sense for a criminal act.

**Date rape** — The crime of forced sexual activity with another person against his or her will. The perpetrator knows the victim.

**Defense of excuse** — Defense based on the idea that the defendant did commit a crime but was not responsible for his or her actions. This is usually seen in insanity defenses.

**Defense of justification** — Defense based on the idea that the defendant did commit a crime, but under the circumstances, he or she was right to do it. This usually applies in cases of self-defense.

**Disorderly conduct** — Disturbing the public peace; usually involves fighting.

**Drug trafficking** — The crime of selling, trading, storing, transporting, or exporting an illegal substance.

**Due process of law** — Fair legal procedures guaranteed by the U.S. Constitution, Amendments 5 and 14.

**Duress** — The defense of being forced to commit a crime against your will.

**Embezzlement** — The crime of legally gaining possession of someone else's property and then converting it for your own use.

**Entrapment** — Actions by a law enforcement agent that persuade a defendant to commit a crime that he or she ordinarily would not commit.

**Extortion** — Taking another person's property (including money) by making threats to harm the person.

**False imprisonment** — The crime of preventing another person from his or her freedom to go where he or she wishes to go.

**Felony** — A serious crime punishable by one year or more in prison.

**Felony murder** — A death that occurs during the commission of a felony, whether intentional or not.

**Fence** — A person who knowingly sells stolen property for profit.

**First-degree murder** — Premeditated, deliberate killing of another person with malice.

**Forgery** — The crime of making false documents or changing genuine documents for profit.

**Good time** — Time that may be deducted from an inmate's sentence for a record of good behavior while incarcerated.

**Grand larceny** — The most severe type of theft of another person's valuable property.

*Habeas corpus* — Latin term meaning "you have the body." A writ of habeas corpus is a mandate usually used when a defendant claims he or she is being held by law enforcement illegally.

**Hate crime** — The crime of harming another person based upon hatred of that person's race, gender, sexual orientation, national origin, or religion.

**Homicide** — The crime of taking the life of another person.

**Identity theft** — The crime of stealing another person's identity to gain something of value.

**Imminent danger** — The element in a self-defense excuse where the defendant fears that injury or death is about to happen immediately.

**Initial aggressor** — A person cannot claim self-defense if he or she started a fight.

**Insanity** — Legal term for when a person is excused for having committed a crime because a mental illness or defect impairs his or her criminal intent to commit the crime. This is not a medical term.

**Involuntary intoxication** — A legal defense based on the defendant being forced or tricked into intoxication.

**Irresistible impulse** — A legal defense based on the idea that a defendant had an impairment of his or her will, making it impossible for him or her to control the impulse to commit a crime.

**Joyriding** — The crime of taking another person's car without intending to keep it permanently or sell it.

**Justifiable homicide** — Killing in self-defense; the death penalty; and use of deadly force by law enforcement officers, including correctional officers.

**Kidnapping** — The crime of carrying away another person against his or her will with the intention of depriving him or her of personal freedom.

**Larceny** — The crime of taking away another person's property without consent with the intent of permanently depriving the owner of the property.

**Loitering** — Lingering in one place for no apparent purpose. This is often seen before theft or robbery.

**Malicious mischief** — The crime of damaging or destroying another person's property.

**Manslaughter** — The crime of illegally killing another person. This does not contain the elements of malice and/or intent seen in homicide and can be voluntary or involuntary.

**Misdemeanor** — A crime punishable by less than one year in jail or a fine.

**Motive** — The reason a defendant committed a crime; prosecutors no longer have to prove motive to convict a defendant.

**Murder** — The illegal and intentional killing of another person; can be either first-degree (planned in advance) or second-degree (in the heat of passion).

**Patron** — In the crime of prostitution, the patron is the person who pays for sex. This person can also be called a "John."

**Pedophile** — A person whose sexual partner of choice is a pre-puberty child. The pedophile can be either heterosexual or homosexual.

**Perjury** — The crime of telling a lie or making a false written statement after one has legally sworn to tell the truth.

**Petty larceny** — A minor form of stealing based on the low value of the item(s) stolen.

**Preponderance of the evidence** — In civil lawsuits, more than 50 percent of the evidence proves the presence or absence of responsibility for harming another person.

**Promoting prostitution** — The crime of soliciting customers for prostitutes; also called "pimping" or "pandering."

**Rape** — The crime of sexually penetrating another person; "rape by instrumentation" is the crime of using an object to sexually penetrate a victim.

**Reason** — The ability to determine right from wrong.

**Receiving stolen property** — The crime of benefiting from another person's property without having personally taking it.

**Riot** — The crime of disorderly conduct committed by three or more people.

**Robbery** — The crime of taking away another person's property by face-to-face threats of harm or actual harm, intending to permanently deprive the owner of his or her property.

**Simple assault** — The crime of assault and battery without the use of a weapon.

**Smuggling** — The crime of transporting illegal items across national boundaries. This also applies to contraband brought into a prison by an inmate's visitor(s).

**Solicitation** — The crime of trying to get someone to commit a crime.

**Stalking** — The crime of intentionally scaring another person by following, tormenting, or harassing him or her.

**Statutory rape** — The crime of having consensual sex with a person under the age of legal consent. This age varies from state to state.

**Theft** — Combines the crimes of larceny, embezzlement, and gaining another person's property under false pretenses (fraud).

**Uttering** — The crime of intentional use or transfer of false documents. This is usually seen in check forgery, which is called "uttering a false instrument."

**Vagrancy** — The crime of wandering around with no visible means of financial support. This often precedes burglary or robbery.

**Vandalism** — The crime of destroying or damaging public property or another person's property without the owner's consent.

**Weapons offenses** — Crimes that involve the illegal sale, possession, alteration, manufacture, transportation, or use of deadly or dangerous weapons.

**White-collar crimes** — Crimes that occur out of the opportunity to get another person's property that are successful because of the perpetrator's occupation. This is usually seen in the business world, such as "insider trading" in the stock market and computer hacking crimes.

# CRIMINAL PROCEDURE TERMS

**Bench trial** — A criminal trial where the defendant waives his or her right to a jury trial and instead elects to have his or her case decided by the trial judge.

**Beyond a reasonable doubt** — The prosecutor's duty to prove the defendant's guilt not by *any* doubt, but beyond the doubt that a reasonable person would have if he or she was not present during the crime.

**Bills of Rights** — Constitutional guarantees that prevent governmental abuses on the people of the United States. They are the first 10 amendments of the U.S. Constitution.

**Bind over** — A judge's decision that, based on evidence presented by the prosecutor, a criminal case will go to trial.

*Certiorari* — Latin for "to be informed of." A writ of certiorari is a written pleading to the U.S. Supreme Court requesting it to review a case decided by a lower court; granted only if the issue is one of constitutional law rather than a retrial of the facts of the case.

**Charging the jury** — Before a jury deliberates, the judge tells them what law applies in a defendant's case and how to apply the law to the facts. This is often an issue in an appeal.

**Clear and convincing evidence** — More than probable cause, but less than the standard of proving a defendant's guilt beyond a reasonable doubt.

**Counsel** *pro bono* — An attorney who represents a defendant at no charge.

**Court of last resort** — The last court that will hear an inmate's final appeal. Not always the U.S. Supreme Court.

**Crime scene investigator** — An expert in using forensic (technical) skills such as collecting DNA evidence, fingerprints, photographs of the crime scene, and interviewing witnesses to the crime. They are also called "criminalists."

**Criminal complaint** — The formal charges against a defendant.

**Criminal procedure** — The legal methods used to detect, investigate, apprehend, prosecute, convict, and punish criminals.

**Cultural defense** — A defense to a criminal charge where the defendant's culture is taken into account in judging his or her guilt. This is sometimes seen in Islamic "honor killings."

**Custodial interrogation** — The questioning of a suspect in a crime that happens after the suspect has been taken into police custody.

**Custody-related search** — Any search by a law enforcement officer of a suspect in a crime after he or she has been taken into custody; no search warrant is necessary, and any evidence found in the search can be used against the suspect in court.

**Death-qualified jurors** — Jurors who are not opposed to the death penalty for convicted murderers.

**Decision to charge** — A prosecutor's decision to begin formal criminal proceedings against a defendant.

**Deliberate indifference** — A complete, intentional disregard by prison staff members for the safety and health of inmates. Under the Supreme Court case of *Estelle v. Gamble,* the Eighth Amendment protects against cruel and unusual punishment, including denying an inmate protection from harm or adequate medical care.

**Direct evidence** — Evidence that directly proves a fact in a criminal case, such as eyewitness testimony or videotapes. This is often an appeal issue because eye-witness testimony has proven to be frequently unreliable.

**Directed verdict** — A judge's decision, based upon a motion by the prosecutor, that enough evidence exists to convict a defendant without a jury's verdict.

**Dismissal with prejudice** — Occurs when a judge terminates a criminal case and declares that the same charges cannot be re-filed against a suspect.

**Dismissal without prejudice** — As above, but the same charges can be re-filed against the same suspect if new evidence surfaces.

**District attorney** — An elected attorney who, along with his or her assistant DAs, are responsible for representing the people of the state in a criminal trial. This is also called a prosecutor, state's attorney, or county attorney.

**Double jeopardy** — Constitutional protection against a defendant being tried twice for the same crime *at the same level of the justice system;* this does not preclude both criminal and civil trials for the same offense.

**Exclusionary rule** — All evidence illegally obtained by law enforcement officers cannot be admitted at trial. The rule has a great many exceptions and is also called "fruit of the poisonous tree."

**Expert witness** — A person who has special knowledge and/ or skills acknowledged by the judge whose testimony may help the jury reach a verdict on the defendant's guilt. They are is also called "hired guns." Expert testimony can be an appeal issue if an inmate challenges whether the expert really *is* an expert.

**Expressed waiver of rights** — Occurs when a suspect waives any or all of his or her legal rights under *Miranda v. Arizona* and understands the consequences of waiving these rights.

**Fourth Amendment rights** — Refers to illegal searches and seizures by law enforcement officers.

**Frivolous lawsuits** — A lawsuit filed that has no foundation in fact, usually filed by inmates and/or attorneys for publicity or politics. In many jurisdictions, judges can refuse to hear meritless lawsuits and may impose fines on attorneys and inmates who file them because of the tremendous burden they place on an already overcrowded judicial system.

**Grabbable area searches** — Refers to a police officer's right to a warrantless search of a suspect's area of immediate reach; meant to protect officers' safety if a suspect has a weapon within reach.

**Grand jury** — In some jurisdictions, a group of jurors who hear evidence and determine if it is enough to bring the defendant to trial; no attorneys are allowed in grand jury proceedings, nor is the defendant. Other jurisdictions without grand juries have *preliminary hearings* that perform the same job but involve attorneys and the defendant.

**Hearsay testimony** — Refers to evidence not stemming from a witness's personal knowledge but based only on what another person told him or her. Although there are exceptions, hearsay is usually not admissible in court.

**Impeaching a witness** — Occurs when a defense attorney or prosecutor attacks the credibility of a witness in court.

**Inchoate offense** — An offense that has not yet been completed but that the defendant has set in motion. This can be an appeal issue, usually in the case of "contracted" murders where the defendant now cannot prevent from happening for some reason.

**Included offense** — A separate, usually lesser, offense that was committed along with the major offense with which the defendant is charged. The judge instructs the jury as to whether they can consider verdicts on lesser-included offenses.

**Indigent defendants** — Those accused of a crime who cannot afford to hire an attorney to represent them. The *Miranda v.*

*Arizona* and *Gideon v. Wainwright* Supreme Court cases require that an attorney be appointed for them at no charge.

**Inherent coercion** — Tactics used by police officers that are not physically abusive but exert great pressure upon a suspect to reveal information. A serious appeal issue and grounds for a new trial that excludes this evidence.

**Inventory searches** — Warrantless searches of a suspect's personal items when he or she is taken into custody. Officers must list every item found and confiscated, including weapons, drugs, money, and other evidence that can be used against the suspect in court.

**Jury nullification** — Refers to a jury's action in reaching a not-guilty verdict, despite clear proof of guilt. Judges disapprove of this, and it usually occurs in cases where a defendant takes the law into his own hands for a good reason, such as killing his child's molester.

**Knock-and-announce search** — Law enforcement officers with a search warrant must knock on a suspect's door and announce their presence and intentions to search. This is the opposite of a "no-knock" search, where officers fear for their safety or that evidence will be destroyed prior to their entry.

**Landmark case** — A court decision that sets a precedent (new standard) in the application of the law and in the justice system. An example is *Miranda v. Arizona*, the Supreme Court's 1966 decision that established the requirement that suspects under arrest be advised of their constitutional rights — also called "Miranda rights" and "Miranda warnings."

**Lineup** — An identification procedure where a suspect stands in a line with others similar in appearance to determine if a victim or witness can identify him or her as the perpetrator of a crime.

**Mandatory minimum sentence** — Determined by a state's legislature, the trial judge has no choice but to sentence a convicted criminal to a minimum amount of years in prison.

**Mistrial** — A trial that is terminated by the judge and declared invalid because an error was made in the trial that could make it unfair and a violation of the defendant's due process rights. This is often an appeal issue if a judge did *not* declare a mistrial when, by law, he or she should have and the defendant was convicted.

**Mockery of justice standard** — The standard under which a defense attorney can be deemed as ineffective counsel only if the circumstances reduced the trial to a farce.

**Motion to suppress evidence** — A pre-trial defense attorney's motion before the judge to exclude some evidence from the trial; usually happens if the evidence is illegally obtained, irrelevant, or unnecessarily prejudicial against the defendant.

*Nolo contendre* — Latin for "I do not wish to contend." A plea by the defendant that accepts the evidence in his or her case but does not admit to the charges against him or her. This is also called a "no contest" plea.

**Opening statements** — Each attorney tells the jury what their evidence will be in the trial and how they intend to prove it. Conversely, the closing arguments are a summary of what evidence each side presented and what the jury's verdict should be.

**Plain view doctrine** — If evidence is in the plain view of a police officer, he or she can seize it without a warrant to be used against the defendant at trial.

**Post-conviction relief (or remedy)** — Procedures that are sought by a convicted person to challenge, in court, the lawfulness of the judgment of guilt, the penalty, or the actions of a corrections institution. This is not the same as an appeal to a higher court.

*Prima facie* — Latin term meaning that the prosecution has presented enough elements of the crime at trial to warrant a jury's deliberation; if this burden is not met, the defense attorney will make a motion to dismiss the case.

**Probable cause** — Enough evidence exists against a suspect for the police to arrest him or her for a specific crime.

**Probative value** — The degree to which a piece of evidence provides something important and is relevant in a criminal trial. This can be an appeal issue if the judge allows evidence that has no probative value but influences the jury's finding of a guilty verdict.

*Pro se* — Latin term for defendants who represent themselves. In cases involving serious crimes, the trial judge may appoint a legal adviser for the defendant.

**Public defenders** — State-employed attorneys who represent defendants who cannot afford to hire a private attorney.

**Racial profiling** — Any law enforcement action that relies on a suspect's race, ethnicity, or national origin to believe that he or she is likely to have committed a crime. This is a hotly disputed topic and a frequent issue on appeal.

**Reasonable Fourth Amendment clause** — This clause bans unreasonable searches and seizures by police officers. The "warrant clause" outlines when arrest and search warrants must be obtained through a judge.

**Released on recognizance** — ROR refers to defendants who are released from custody without having to post bail. The judge determines that the defendant is not a flight risk.

*Res ipsa loquitor* — Latin for "the thing speaks for itself." For example, choke marks on a murder victim's neck indicates that he or she was strangled to death. This can be an appeal issue if an expert witness incorrectly applies it in a criminal trial.

**Restitution** — Money paid to an inmate's victim that he or she earns while in prison. It is usually ordered by the judge and is looked on favorably by parole boards.

**Reversible error** — An error in law made by a lower court trial judge that could have affected the outcome of the case. This is the opposite of "harmless error."

**Revocation hearing** — A hearing before a judge or parole board to decide if a person on parole or probation has violated the terms of his or her release and should be returned to prison or jail.

**Rules of evidence** — Legal rules that determine whether evidence can or cannot be admitted at a trial. A frequent appeal issue if a judge allowed evidence to be unlawfully presented to a jury.

**Seizure** — The physical taking of property belonging to a criminal suspect. This may require a warrant, especially in cases of invasive procedures like blood and DNA samples.

**Self-incrimination clause** — Part of the Fifth Amendment that guarantees that a defendant cannot be forced to be witnesses against themselves during police questioning or trial.

**Sneak and peak searches** — Warrants that allow police officers to enter a suspect's private home without the suspect's consent or knowledge. Evidence obtained may be used against a defendant at trial. Also called a *delayed notification* search.

***Stare decisis*** — Latin for "stand by the decision," a legal principle that requires courts to be bound to their decisions in previous similar cases; an appeal issue if this principle is not followed.

**Statutes of limitation** — Laws that specify the length of time permitted to lapse between the commission of a crime and the prosecution of that crime; cases can be dismissed if the statute has lapsed, although crimes like child abuse are exceptions, and there is no statute of limitation on first-degree murder or treason.

**Stop and frisk** — The power of a police officer to stop a person and briefly examine his or her body surface or clothing to discover weapons, contraband, and other things that may be related to a crime. It is a legal warrantless search *only* if the officer believes the person may have committed or is about to commit a crime.

**Strickland standard** — refers to a case decided by the U.S. Supreme Court about what constitutes "inadequate counsel." This is frequently the subject of an appeal when a defendant claims his lawyer was incompetent in his or her handling of the case. If a case does not meet the Strickland standard of adequate counsel, the appeal is likely to be successful.

**Three-strikes laws** — Laws that require mandatory prison sentences — including life without parole — for offenders who are convicted of a third felony.

**Venue** — The location (city or county) where a criminal trial is held. Defense attorneys can make a change of venue motion if they believe the defendant cannot receive a fair trial in the "home" venue — this can become an issue on appeal.

*Voir dire* — French term meaning "to speak the truth," which refers to the prosecutor and defense attorney's examination of prospective jurors to excuse those who cannot be unbiased in reaching a verdict.

**Voluntary intoxication** — Consuming alcohol and/or other drugs prior to committing a crime. This is never a legal defense.

**Writ** — A document issued by a judge either ordering or forbidding the performance of a certain act.

# Appendix B:
# Common Prison Slang

**Ace dude** — A best friend.

**Adjustment segregation (ADJ)** — A form of solitary confinement for punishment of a prison rule violation.

**ADMAX** — Administrative maximum; used in the federal prison system to describe the highest security level. This is also called a "super-max" prison.

**Aryan** — A white supremacy member of the Aryan Brotherhood.

**Back to back** — An inmate who is serving more than one sentence for more than one crime consecutively (one after another) rather than concurrently (all sentences served at one time).

**Baked** — High on prescription drugs given by the prison physician.

**Beatdown** — A violent assault upon another inmate.

**Biker** — A term for white motorcycle outlaw gangs; also known as crackers, peckerwoods, honkies, or rednecks by non-whites.

**Biscuit** — A woman.

**Billy** — A white inmate.

**Bit** — An inmate's sentence.

**Bones** — Playing dice or dominoes.

**Bone yard** — The conjugal visit rooms.

**Bootlicker** — An inmate "snitch" or one who is being too friendly with the COs.

**Boss** — A corrections officer; also called "hacks."

**Bounce** — Leaving the prison on parole.

**Box** — A radio, a fight, segregation, or a woman.

**Bragging rights** — The winner of a fight between inmates.

**Break camp** — To run, to get away from a situation.

**Bring the drama/bring it** — An invitation to fight.

**Bump it** — Stop what you are doing.

**Bush bandit** — A child molester; also called a "Chester."

**Cage or crib** — A cell.

**Captain Jack** — Heroin.

**Cat J** — An inmate in obvious need of psychiatric medication.

**Catwalk** — An elevated walkway patrolled by COs that covers cells, gyms, and hallways, giving them a wider view of a prison's area.

**Cave dweller** — An inmate who spends most of his time inside his cell out of fear of being victimized in some way. Also called "Vikings."

**Cellie** — An inmate's cell mate; also called a "roomie."

**Check** — An inmate telling another to check his behavior for disrespect.

**Cherry** — A female inmate who has not been "initiated" into lesbian prison sex.

**Chillin'** — Relaxing.

**Chronic** — Marijuana.

**C-note** — A hundred dollar bill.

**Cobras** — A Latino gang.

**Corner** — The area where inmates meet their visitors.

**Crank** — An inmate who is hard to get along with; also a slang name for methamphetamine.

**Crash gate** — An electrically controlled gate in a prison hallway that controls inmates' movements within the prison.

**Dead man** — An inmate on death row awaiting execution.

**Dayroom** — An area of a unit where inmates can watch TV and play cards, dominoes, and board games.

**Desert boots** — Footwear issued by the prison; favored among the Aryan Brotherhood.

**Dig?** — Understand?

**Dipping** — Getting into another inmate's business.

**Disciples** — An African American gang; also called Gangster Disciples.

**D.R.** — Disciplinary report for misconduct written by a staff member; also called a "write-up," "shot," and a "ticket."

**Dog (Dawg)** — A friend, buddy.

**Do not get tore off** — Do not allow yourself to become a victim.

**Dotted eye** — A black eye resulting from a fight.

**Drag** — A lie or excuse.

**Ear hustling** — Listening to other inmates' conversations.

**Entertain me** — Talk to me.

*Ese* — An inmate of Hispanic origin; an insult when used by a non-Hispanic.

**Featherwood** — A white inmate's woman.

**Feel ya/smell ya/hear ya** — Understanding the point of another inmate's conversation.

**Femme** — A female inmate who assumes the submissive role in a lesbian relationship.

**Five-O** — A warning to other inmates that a CO is coming; also called "fire in the hole" and "man walking."

**Fish** — A young, first-time inmate; also called "fresh meat."

**Flatten out** — An inmate's release date when he has completed his sentence.

**Fort** — The prison.

**Freeze me** — Never talk to me again.

**Froggy** — An inmate who feels like fighting.

**Funk** — Cool, relaxed, or smelly.

**Game** — Conning other inmates and staff.

**Gangbanger** — A gang member.

**Geek-up** — Encouraging one inmate to fight another inmate.

**Gen pop** — General population; usually minimum security within a unit, in the mainstream.

**Get some business** — Leave me alone, go away.

**Gladiator school** — A unit that houses young and very violent inmates.

**Gorilla** — An inmate who takes what he wants from other inmates.

**Green leaf** — Marijuana.

**Hanging paper** — Forging documents, usually checks.

**Hanging tough** — Being cool during hard times in prison.

**High-tech shit** — When an inmate has a good drug-related plan.

**Hook** — An inmate who intentionally starts fights, usually among gangs.

**Home team** — An inmate's group of friends; also called "homies."

**Hootch** — Inmate-made alcohol; also called "volcano juice" and "pruno."

**House** — An inmate's cell.

**Jacking** — Stealing.

**Jailhouse lawyer** — An inmate who studies the law through the prison's law library and helps others with their appeals, motions for new trials, and other legal issues.

**Jewelry** — Handcuffs, shackles.

**Kicking it** — Relaxing, talking with other inmates.

**Kick it in** — Give up your property.

**Lame** — A weak, phony story or action.

**Latin Kings** — A Latino gang.

**L-ball** — Serving a life sentence.

**Lightweight** — An inmate who has little or no influence over other inmates.

**List** — A written record of inmates who owe other inmates money for contraband.

**Living large** — Having money to spend at the prison commissary.

**Lockdown** — A security action where all inmates are locked in their cells to stop or prevent violence.

**Lock-n-sock** — A bar of soap wrapped in the toe of a sock to be used as a weapon.

**Main line** — The line in the chow hall that is open to the general inmate population; the "short line" is for kitchen staff to eat before all other inmates.

**Man up** — Take responsibility for your actions, or have courage.

**Man walking** — A phrase that means a CO is coming.

**Mark** — An inmate or staff member to be conned and manipulated.

**Max mentality** — A violent way of thinking and acting that is used as a survival technique in prison; also called "Beirut mode."

**Mean mugging** — Giving another inmate an intimidating look.

**Moon cricket** — A racial slur by white inmates toward African Americans.

**New boot** — A rookie CO.

**Open up a can of whoop-ass** — Starting a fight.

**OPP** — Other peoples' problems; stay out of them.

**Package** — A bundle of drugs smuggled into the prison.

**Pat search** — When a CO searches the outer clothes of an inmate.

**Perp** — Perpetrator.

**Player** — An inmate who "plays the game" on others.

**Play it off** — Act like you understand.

**Pour salt on someone's back** — gossiping about another inmate.

**PRC** — Program Review Committee; a four-member team that reassesses custody and security levels and work assignments every six months.

**Program segregation** — A high-custody level that a new inmate is placed in while he or she is being classified.

**Propers** — Giving respect to another inmate; also called "props."

**Pruno** — The name given to alcohol secretly made by inmates in prison.

**Punk** — A weak or gay inmate.

**Pusher** — An inmate who is instructed, or volunteers, to help a wheelchair-bound inmate; not the same as a drug pusher (seller).

**Putting your business on the street** — Talking too much.

**Real crime** — Murder, armed robbery, or aggravated assault. Inmates often look up to those who committed these crimes.

**Rep** — An inmate's reputation among other inmates.

**Riding the lightning** — Execution by electrocution.

**Riding the needle** — Execution by lethal injection.

**Riding the train** — Getting high.

**Ringout** — An alarm bell that sounds when inmates are leaving the unit for their work assignments.

**Roll the doors** — A command from one CO to another to open or close cell doors in a unit.

**Roll right** — Tobacco.

**Royals** — A white prison gang.

**Runner** — A trusted inmate with the job of delivering papers to and from staff.

**Safe** — A woman inmate's term for her vagina, where contraband is often hidden.

**Seg** — Segregation; also known as "the hole."

**Send-out** — Sending money to someone outside the prison to buy drugs.

**Senior** — The prison's security chief.

**Shackles** — Leg irons that go around both ankles with a bar in the middle that is attached to handcuffs; they are used to prevent an inmate from escaping or harming others.

**Shank** — A prison-made sharp weapon used for cutting or stabbing others.

**Shot-caller** — An inmate, usually a gang leader, who makes decisions about what others can and cannot do.

**Slick** — An inmate who is good at manipulating other inmates and staff.

**Smashed** — Beat down in a fight.

**Snap** — Going crazy, out of control.

**Snitch** — An inmate who gains favors from COs by revealing information about the plans and activities of other inmates; they are at serious risk for being harmed and often housed in administrative segregation for their safety.

**Spread your cheeks** — Showing a CO your buttocks during a strip search to make sure you are not hiding contraband in your rectum.

**Square John** — An inmate who does not belong to a prison gang.

**Stash** — To hide something.

**Stand-up guy** — An inmate who can be trusted.

**Store** — Inmates selling contraband from their cells.

**Straight** — Telling the truth; also called "straight up."

**Stud broad or daddy** — A female inmate who assumes the dominant role in lesbian activities.

**Strip search** — Occurs when an inmate is searched while naked by a CO to detect contraband and/or weapons.

**Sucker-punched** — Getting hit by another inmate without seeing it coming.

**Sunshine** — Matches or cigarette lighters.

**Sweat some tears** — Having a hard time or a bad day.

**Taxation** — Being robbed by another inmate.

**Tender** — A weak inmate.

**Throw-down** — A fight or brawl, usually between rival gangs.

**Throwing dirt** — Talking badly about someone.

**Tired** — Expressing dislike for someone.

**Tits** — Slang term for heroin; smuggled into prison by mail or visitors.

**TLU** — Temporary lock-up; used for minor disciplinary action or while a major infraction is being investigated by COs.

**Tree-jumper** — A rapist on the streets.

**Tree-jumper school** — An area of the prison that houses sex offenders.

**Turn out** — To make another inmate into a sexual punk.

**UA** — Urinalysis lab work that detects drugs and alcohol in the body.

**Vice Lords** — An African American gang.

**Wack** — Describes something either good or bad.

**Wam-wam** — Junk food; also called "zoom-zoom."

**Wanna-be** — A follower of a shot-caller.

**When the bars break** — When cell doors open.

**Wild West** — A violent place on the streets or in prison.

**Wigger** — A white inmate who acts African American.

**Wolf** — A male inmate who assumes the dominate role in homosexual relationships.

**Yo-yo** — Getting someone's attention.

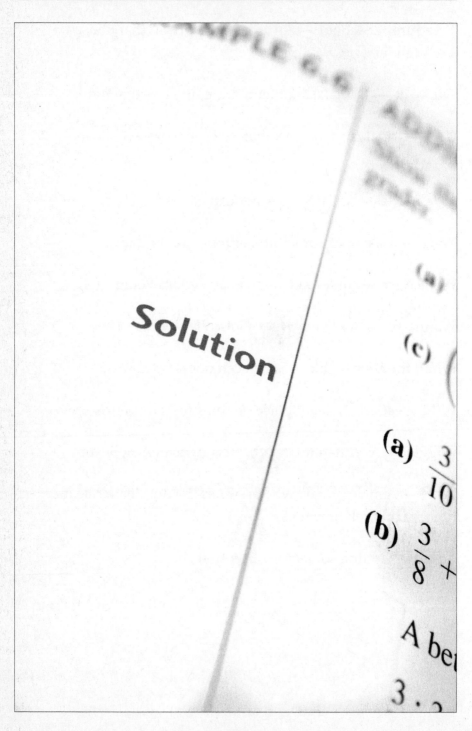

# Appendix C: Answers to "Check Your Understanding" Questions

## Check Your Understanding No. 1

1. True or False: Criminal law determines what actions are, and are not, illegal. **TRUE**

2. True or False: Criminal procedure determines how the justice system works for people who are accused of a crime. **TRUE**

## Check Your Understanding No. 2

1. True or False: One of your Miranda rights is to have a speedy trial. **TRUE**

2. True or False: In criminal law, a felony crime is more serious than a misdemeanor crime. **TRUE**

3. True or False: An arraignment is part of criminal procedure. **TRUE**

4. True or False: Your Miranda rights do not apply once you go to prison. **FALSE**

## Check Your Understanding No. 3

1. True or False: "Jail" and "prison" are the same thing. **FALSE**

2. True or False: In the case study, Tom committed a felony. **TRUE**

3. True or False: Once you are in prison, you no longer need a lawyer. **FALSE**

4. True or False: Only the facts of your case are important; your attitude and behavior in court plays no part in your court proceedings. **FALSE**

## Check Your Understanding No. 5

1. True or False: A prison is a small community within a city, a larger community. **TRUE**

2. True or False: The classification team determines when you will be released from prison. **FALSE**

3. True or False: Custody levels and security levels are the same thing. **FALSE**

4. True or False: It is unlikely that you will ever meet the prison warden or deputy warden. **FALSE**

5. True or False: The primary duties of corrections officers are custody and control. **TRUE**

## Check Your Understanding No. 6

1. True or False: Every inmate has a right to have a prison job to help support his family. **FALSE**

2. True or False: Once you enter prison, you no longer need an attorney to represent you. **FALSE**

3. True or False: You cannot be legally charged with a crime you commit in prison. **FALSE**

4. Being "indigent" means that you lack the ability to pay court costs and attorney's fees. **TRUE**

5. Your appeal or motion for a new trial should be based upon the jury's misconduct in your case. **FALSE**

## Check Your Understanding No. 7

1. True or False: You will not need to take your medical records because the prison physician will rely upon your own health knowledge. **FALSE**

2. True or False: Always tell your prison doctor about any pre-existing health conditions. **TRUE**

3. True or False: Even if you do not smoke, you can bring a lighter into the prison. **FALSE**

4. True or False: Arranging for emotional support for your family is an important part of your rehabilitation. **TRUE**

5. True or False: Studies have shown that when an inmate is paroled, the most important issue is whether he or she goes home to a caring, stable home life. **TRUE**

## Check Your Understanding No. 8

1. True or False: When you are uncertain about a rule. consult a CO and/or your inmate handbook. **TRUE**

2. True or False: The "Convict Code" is an informal set of rules designed by inmates about how to live in prison. **TRUE**

3. True or False: "Count times" refers to the length of your sentence. **FALSE**

4. True or False: It is your friends' and family's responsibility to learn about prison mail rules. **FALSE**

5. True or False: You receive one warning if you are off-limits before you get a write-up for doing it again. **FALSE**

## Check Your Understanding No. 9

1. True or False: You can use your recreation time to create crafted items that you can sell in prison-run stores. **TRUE**

2. True or False: Recreation yards are a good place to settle scores against rival gang members. **FALSE**

3. True or False: You are not allowed to make phone calls to anyone but family members. **FALSE**

4. True or False: Your visitors must be approved by a background check before they are allowed to see you. **TRUE**

5. True or False: Displays of physical affection are against the rules in every U.S. federal or state prison. **TRUE**

## Check Your Understanding No. 10

1. True or False: Jail conditions are pretty much the same as prison conditions. **FALSE**

2. True or False: If you see a crowd of inmates gathering, go and join them to see what it is all about.     **FALSE**

3. True or False: The only person you can really trust in prison is your cellie.     **FALSE**

4. True or False: The best way to establish your "rep" is to talk tough when you first arrive in prison.     **FALSE**

5. True or False: Mentally ill inmates are no danger to others because they take medications.     **FALSE**

## Check Your Understanding No. 11

1. True or False: Gangs that are active outside prison are not active inside prison.     **FALSE**

2. True or False: Prison gangs are formed around race and ethnic backgrounds.     **TRUE**

3. True or False: The most dangerous gang today in prison is the Aryan Brotherhood.     **TRUE**

4. True or False: Since gangs are suspicious of strangers, it is unlikely that you will be approached about joining a gang.     **FALSE**

5. True or False: Prison gangs are mostly made up of "long-termers" who do not expect to be paroled.     **TRUE**

## Check Your Understanding No. 12

1. True or False: All alcohol in prison comes from "outside."     **FALSE**

2. True or False: Decongestants are the only drugs abused by inmates.     **FALSE**

3. True or False: PREA legislation prevents all forms of prison rape.     **FALSE**

4. True or False: Rape is mostly an act of power, not just a sex act.     **TRUE**

5. True or False: The best way to prevent yourself from being sexually assaulted is to know and follow all prison rules about safety.     **TRUE**

## Check Your Understanding No.13

1. True or False: Corrections officers today have no formal training in their jobs. **FALSE**

2. True or False: Just being polite and respectful will help you get along with COs. **TRUE**

3. True or False: Extreme thinking can lead to poor choices and decisions. **TRUE**

4. True or False: Learning racism and hatred will not help you get released from prison. **TRUE**

5. True or False: Thinking about your own background can help you become more tolerant of people who are different from you. **TRUE**

## Check Your Understanding No. 14

1. True or False: One of the main challenges in prison medicine is overcrowding. **TRUE**

2. True or False: You cannot fire your prison physician. **TRUE**

3. True or False: Court cases have failed to review the medical care of inmates. **FALSE**

4. True or False: A kite is a form inmates use to request a medical appointment. **TRUE**

5. True or False: The Athens Oath was designed to insure adequate medical for inmates. **TRUE**

## Check Your Understanding No. 15

1. True or False: Inmates can volunteer to help others with medical issues such as difficulty walking. **TRUE**

2. True or False: Compassionate release for terminally ill inmates is always granted. **FALSE**

3. True or False: The only types of alcohol and drug programs in prison today are 12-step programs. **TRUE**

4. True or False: Elderly inmates rarely have their medical needs met. **FALSE**

5.  True or False: Medical treatment for alcohol and other drug abuse is available in prison. **FALSE**

## Check Your Understanding No.16

1.  True or False: You should not tell your children that you are in prison so they will not worry about you. **FALSE**

2.  True or False: You cannot be an active part of your child's life while you are in prison. **FALSE**

3.  True or False: Ongoing contact with your family is the most important factor in whether or not you will reunite with them when you are released from prison. **TRUE**

4.  True or False: Incarcerated parents and their very young children need to touch each other often to create a bond between them. **TRUE**

5.  True or False: Writing letters is not helpful in keeping inmates involved in their children's lives. **FALSE**

## Check Your Understanding No. 17

1.  True or False: Your children are undergoing as much stress as you are while you are in prison. **TRUE**

2.  True or False: If your parental rights are terminated, your children are no longer interested in finding you. **FALSE**

3.  True or False: Because you have committed crimes, your children are genetically destined to also commit crimes and be incarcerated. **FALSE**

4.  True or False: All foster care homes are uncaring and brutal toward the children placed with them. **FALSE**

5.  True or False: Inmates who have committed sexual assaults against minors could have their parental rights terminated. **TRUE**

## Check Your Understanding No. 18

1.  True or False: Your spouse or partner needs your emotional support while you are in prison. **TRUE**

2.  True or False: Jealous behavior on your part will show your partner how much you still love him or her. **FALSE**

3.  True or False: It is your partner's responsibility to meet all your needs while you are in prison. **FALSE**

4.  True or False: It is always your parents' fault that you are in prison because they failed to raise you correctly. **FALSE**

5.  True or False: Because of Hollywood stereotypes, your parents will fear for your safety while you are in prison. **TRUE**

## Check Your Understanding No. 19

1.  True or False: More women are convicted of drug-related offenses than any other crime. **TRUE**

2.  True or False: It is not possible for you to maintain a bond with your children during your incarceration. **FALSE**

3.  True or False: You can help rehabilitate yourself by participating in therapy and educational programs. **TRUE**

4.  True or False: In most cases, women give birth in the prison hospital. **FALSE**

5.  True or False: Many female inmates were abused during their childhoods. **TRUE**

## Check Your Understanding No. 20

1.  True or False: If you go to prison, you will automatically lose custody of your children. **FALSE**

2.  True or False: In most cases, it is better for your children to be placed with a relative while you are incarcerated. **TRUE**

3.  True or False: Your wishes will be taken into consideration regarding the care and custody of your children. **TRUE**

4.  True or False: Women are safer from sexual assaults in prison than in the past. **TRUE**

5.  True or False: Every skill you have can be taught to other inmates. **TRUE**

## Check Your Understanding No. 21

1. True or False: When you surrender your freedom, you also surrender your dignity.  **FALSE**

2. True or False: "Prisonization" means becoming accustomed to the way of life in prison.  **TRUE**

3. True or False: Putting your time in prison to good use will help you to keep your mind right.  **TRUE**

4. True or False: You are not allowed to attend church services or study holy books in prison.  **FALSE**

5. True or False: If you start or participate in a prison riot, you cannot be charged with any crime because you are already incarcerated.  **FALSE**

# Bibliography

Anonymous, A. (1980 revised). *Alcoholics Anonymous: The Big Book*. New York: Alcoholics Anonymous.

Bernstein, N. (2005). *All Alone in the World: Children of the Incarcerated*. New York: The New Press.

Fontana, T. (2003). *Oz: Behind These Walls, The Journal of Augustus Hill*. New York: Harper Collins Publishers, Inc.

Golden, R. (2005). *War on the Family: Mothers in Prison and the Families They Leave Behind (Kindle Edition)*. New York: Routledge, Taylor and Francis Group.

Hazelden. (2002). *Criminal and Addictive Thinking*. Center City: Hazelden Publishing Educational Services.

Kohut, M. (2005, April 14). Killers Among Us. *Criminal Justice* , p. 3.

Levinthal, C. (2006). *Drugs, Society and Criminal Justice*. Boston: Pearson Education, Inc.

Martone, C. (2005). *Loving Though Bars: Children with Parents in Prison*. Santa Monica: Santa Monica Press, LLC.

Jones, R. (1987). *Disorderly Conduct: Verbatim Excerpts from Actual Cases*. New York: Norton.

Samaha, J. (2005). *Criminal Law*. Belmont: Thompson Learning, Inc.

Samaha, J. (2005). *Criminal Procedure*. Belmont: Thompson Learning, Inc.

Santos, M. G. (2004). *About Prison*. Belmont: Thompson Learning, Inc.

Santos, M. G. (2006). *Inside: Life Behind Bars in America*. New York: St. Martin's Press.

Schmalleger, F. (2008). *Criminal Justice Today: An Introductory Text for the 21st Century*. Upper Saddle River: Pearson, Prentice Hall.

Sevilla, C. M. (1992). *Disorder in the Court: Great Fractured Moments in Courtroom History*. New York: Norton.

Shaffer, V. A. (2007 e-book). *I Hear Your Cry: Women in Prison*. Lincoln, NE: iUniverse.

Talvi, S. (2007). *Women Behind Bars: The Crisis of Women in the U.S. Prison System*. Emeryville, CA: Seal Press.

Tayoun, J. (2002). *Going to Prison?* Brunswick: Biddle.

Toch, H. &. (2002). *Acting Out: Maladaptive Behavior in Confinement*. Washinton, D.C.: American Psychological Association.

Trimpey, J. (1989). *The Small Book: A Revolutionary Alternative For Overcoming Alcohol and Drug Dependance*. New York: Lotus Press.

# Author Biography

Margaret Kohut is an Oklahoma native and still holds proudly to her "Midwestern drawl." She earned bachelor's degrees in English and criminal justice, and a master's degree in social work. Her initial foray into human service work was as a correctional officer in both adult and juvenile maximum security correctional institutions. Margaret's unique job history includes being a courtroom bailiff and a fugitive recovery agent ("bounty hunter"), and she spent a year in the private practice of clinical social work specializing in adoption studies, pre-sentence investigations, probation and parole intervention, family therapy, and therapy with troubled juveniles. Margaret has a strong educational and vocational history of forensic counseling and addiction therapy.

Margaret served in the United States Air Force for 17 years as a commissioned officer and clinical social worker, providing psychotherapy services for active duty members, family members, and retirees. Margaret served the nation during Operation Desert Storm and Operation Iraqi Freedom. She is now a disabled veteran, conducting her full-time freelance writing business from her home. Margaret maintains national-level certifications in human services. She is a prolific writer, having penned many award-winning publications for the Air Force on mental health issues, domestic violence, workplace violence, chemical dependency, trauma therapy, and adolescent acting-out behavior. As a civilian, Margaret coauthored an academic textbook on sexual serial killers and has been extensively published in the *Canadian Journal of Adlerian Psychology* and other academic publications. Margaret founded Rocky Mountain Way Freelance Writing in February 2006 after more than 20 years of non-commercial writing. Margaret was selected for the 2007-2008 Cambridge Registry Honors Edition of Outstanding Business and Professional Women. She is the recipient of numerous writing awards, including the 2008 National Book Award and the Bronze Medal Award from the Independent Publishers contest in 2008 for her book on school bullying. In 2009, Margaret was selected for lifetime inclusion in the Cambridge Who's Who Registry.

Margaret lives in Anaconda, Montana with her husband of 18 years, Lt. Col. (ret) Dr. Tristan Kohut, senior physician at the Montana State Prison, and their 13 miniature dachshunds; most of them are accomplished animal-assisted therapy dogs. She can be reached via her Web site, **www.rockymountainwaywriting.com**.

# Index

# R

# S

# T

# V

# W